Blow Your Own Horn

Other Books by Jeffrey P. Davidson

Marketing Your Consulting and Professional Services (with
    Richard A. Connor, Jr.)
Checklist Management: The Eight-Hour Manager
Marketing Your Community
Marketing to the Fortune 500
Getting New Clients (with Richard A. Connor, Jr.)
Look Before You Leap

Blow Your Own Horn

How to Market Yourself and Your Career

JEFFREY P. DAVIDSON

American Management Association

This book is available at a special
discount when ordered in bulk quantities.
For information, contact Special Sales Department,
AMACOM, a division of American Management Association,
135 West 50th Street, New York, NY 10020.

Library of Congress Cataloging-in-Publication Data

Davidson, Jeffrey P.
  Blow your own horn.

  Includes index.
  1. Career development. 2. Professions–Marketing.
I. Title.
HF5549.5.C35D375   1987   650.1′4   86-47809
ISBN 0-8144-5908-0

Printing number

10 9 8 7 6 5 4 3 2 1

This book is dedicated to my five mentors—H. Edward Muendel, Richard A. Connor, Jr., Robert Bookman, Dave Yoho, and Herman Holtz; to my career coach— Penny Garner; and to my good friend and "life coach"—Betty R. Arbuckle.

Acknowledgments

There are many people I would like to thank who helped in the preparation of this book. Dianne L. Walbrecker and Katherine J. Reynolds made key conceptual and editorial contributions. Robert Bird, Louis Baron, and Ziad Baradi helped in collecting research, editing, and proofing.

I would also like to thank Karl Weber, whose enthusiasm for the project made it a "go," and Peter Schneider for his astute marketing input and support. Thanks to Nancy Brandwein, Therese Mausser, Janet Frick, and Eva Weiss. Thanks also to Dr. Janet G. Elsea, Lou Hampton, Margaret Bedrosian, Dr. Harry L. Olsen, Andrew Jenkins-Murphy, Arnold "Nick" Carter, and Patricia McCallum for their contributions to specific chapters.

Finally, I would like to thank Judy Dubler for her usual excellent word processing support.

Jeffrey P. Davidson

Contents

Introduction
Why Career
Marketing?

When people first hear about the concept of career marketing, their reaction is often one of surprise. "Am I supposed to sell myself like a box of cereal?" they may ask. "Is self-marketing really necessary? If I'm bright, ambitious, and hard-working, won't I rise to the top of my career ladder without any special marketing effort?"

Increasingly, the answer to the last question is no. Those of us in the baby boom generation, born between 1946 and 1958, are part of the largest "generational cohort" in history. As a result, we've been up against significant competition at every stage of our lives—getting into a good college, finding that first job, locating an affordable apartment, meeting the right mate, and so on. Under the circumstances, maintaining a competitive advantage isn't just a good idea—it's a necessity. And self-marketing is a vital part of that effort.

This book acknowledges and explores the notions that you

must be your own career coach; that career marketing is a continuous process; that the continued development of interpersonal skills supports career advancement; and that, for many people, professional exposure is the fastest ticket to the top.

Controlling Your Own Career

Where is the locus of control for your career? Is it your boss, your parents, the government, your spouse, your peers? Let's agree right now that you and you alone are in control of your career. Frequently, people tell me how a difficult boss held them back, or how they simply did not have time to write an article, or how they "never have been very good" at networking. Such statements only shift the blame for not reaching career goals onto others or onto "inherent" traits.

In the short run, you certainly can be the victim of a bad organization or a bad boss and, in the short run, there are certainly good reasons why you could not take the proactive step that would help propel your career. In the long run, however, there are simply no excuses. *You* are in control of your career; it does not control you.

Planting the Seeds Early

As a general principle, the earlier you set goals, make a commitment, and take action, the greater the long-term results. Yet, there is no use in bemoaning the fact that you never really set goals previously, or that you wasted the last three years in a dead-end job. *Today* is the future you were thinking about six years ago. That time has come and gone. Will what you are doing six years from now be supported by action that you initiate today?

Contemporary society, unfortunately, propels us faster and faster toward immediate gratification. Long-term planning, goal setting, sacrifice, and patience seem rare in a generation that wants to "have it all," "do it all," and have it and do it all *now*. The article you write next week may not be accepted for another couple of months and may not be published until a year from now. The groups you called about a speaking engagement may not return your call for several weeks or months, and may not schedule a date until the middle of next year.

Few of the career marketing activities discussed in this book offer big immediate payoffs (although some of them definitely do). Successful career marketers must realize that careers have a long life—30, maybe 40 years—and that you must balance short- and long-term activities to take care of what must be done today, and to facilitate what you choose to do tomorrow.

Career professionals who recognize the one-to-one ratio of effort and accomplishment view their careers not simply in terms of today, next week, or next year, but as a long, unfolding journey. These professionals have a definite edge over the rest.

Sharon Louise Connelly, Ph.D., in her brilliant forthcoming book *"Work Spirit": Recapturing the Vitality of Work*, observes that "individuals demonstrating work spirit have a sense that everything that they have ever done contributes to what they are working toward."

The Rules of Reality

Reality is not what you or I think it is. It simply is what it is, and the more closely we can manage our careers in accordance with reality, the greater the return for our efforts. The great salesman and motivational speaker Earl Nightingale says, "It is easier to adjust ourselves to the hardships of a poor living than it is to adjust ourselves to the hardships of making a better one." This reality applies to individuals, communities, regions, and even entire countries. It also helps explain why, when we attempt to move from where we are, often we end up settling for where we started from.

My own tendency to "accept the hardship of a poor living"

was brought home to me after I won a large and prestigious consulting contract several years ago. My deputy project manager and I plotted 109 steps for successfully completing the project. This planning session required our full time and attention for two days. At the end of this process, we had created a plan that we knew, down to the marrow in our bones, would work and serve us well. Immediately thereafter, I realized that I should apply the same time and energy to plot the steps required to advance my career. Yet, for three years I was unable even to get started.

If you don't set goals, and you don't pursue them vigorously, no one else will be keeping score; you can continue to get by and maintain the look of prosperity year after year. But in those quiet moments when there is no one to answer to but ourselves, how do we justify procrastinating for years? How do we justify not making the effort to get what we really want or achieve what we really want to achieve?

Barring outrageous misfortune, for the vast majority, life is a self-fulfilling prophesy, and playing it safe, not taking a risk, not going the extra mile, or accepting the hardship of a poor living becomes our fate. The longer we stay in that mode, the harder it is to get out. The only way out is through action.

Becoming an Effective Career Marketer

In many ways, marketing is like life in general. Those who get ahead in life are natural-born marketers. Elected politicians, your company's president, and all those whom society holds in respect somehow mastered the ability to effectively and visibly serve a constituency, shareholders, or other target market.

Whether you were a marketing major in college or have never read one word on the topic, you can become an effective career marketer. Implementing the strategies and recommendations in this book requires no marketing background or aptitude. What is required is the ability to produce a self-definition, set goals to which you are committed, and pursue your goals vigorously.

To become an effective career marketer doesn't mean being boastful, arrogant, pushy, or egotistical; it doesn't mean using other people or employing deceit or trickery. As you'll learn in this book, the most effective self-marketing is done with class and honesty and is based on a genuine respect and concern for the needs of others. As marketing professionals will tell you, without a worthwhile product, no amount of puffery can produce long-term sales. It's the same with career marketing. The secret is simply to develop the skills that will make you a valuable professional and then learn to promote those skills in a way that will earn you the respect and success you deserve.

Each of the following chapters is based on personal experience, including failures and successes, in marketing my own career.

What I am presenting has actually worked for me, and, if aggressively implemented, will work for you as well.

Part I

You Are Your Own Career Coach

Chapter 1

Your Personal Marketing Plan

To defy external forces, to rise above circumstances, is to proclaim the sovereignty of the human spirit.

Chaim Weizmann

Who needs a marketing plan? Everyone! You need a marketing plan to sell products, services, ideas, and, above all, yourself. A concise marketing plan will allow you to focus your time and energy in one direction, thereby increasing your effectiveness. It defines what is offered, to whom, and through what methods. Without a marketing plan, you're likely to keep jousting at windmills.

The marketing plan is an organized, written tool describing

your present career situation, opportunities, and problems, and establishing specific and realistic career goals.

The marketing plan also outlines specific action steps required to accomplish these goals, including a milestone chart.

As a strategic career marketer, one of your chief responsibilities is anticipating changes that will allow you time to act decisively. Since your plan must be changed as the environment and you change, career marketing planning is a continuous process. Let's look at the simplest marketing plan that will get you started, and that works!

The One-Minute Definition

Develop a one-sentence, one-minute definition of what you have to offer or want to offer to the world—a one-sentence "marketing plan." That one sentence, carefully thought out, will point you in the right direction and help focus all your efforts.

This is my own one sentence: "I'm in the business of providing marketing and management assistance to professional service providers and organizations throughout the United States, Western Europe, and Japan through books, speaking engagements, and consulting assignments." That one sentence describes the services I provide, for whom, and how. As time passes, I'll probably revise it.

As a career professional, your one-sentence marketing definition should be realistic, acknowledging your current position and focusing on the future. After establishing your one key sentence, you can turn your attention to setting—and reaching—your goals.

SETTING AND REACHING GOALS

I set goals before dinner. I set goals on planes. I do it when I wasn't even planning to do it. I am forever setting goals—most of which I later discard, but that's okay. The process of goal setting involves much overreaching initially, followed by a sifting through to find the realistic, attainable gems.

When is the best time to pick goals? Whenever they pop up. Or, to put it more scientifically, when you're in a relaxed, creative, contemplative state of mind. Author Napoleon Hill once said that "imagination is the workshop of the mind." To get started in goal setting, open your mind up to the full range of possibilities.

Your Career List

Management consultant Pat McCallum, an author on the subject of goal setting, emphasizes the importance of maintaining a focus in setting your goals. To sift clearly through all those that come up, McCallum outlines several steps.

Draw a line down the center of a blank piece of paper and list the things you want in your career on the left side. Then list the things you *don't want* on the right. Take all the ideas you had when your imagination was running wild and, at this point, pick out those that are reasonable or those that have higher priorities.

A few well-chosen goals that are challenging, yet reachable, are preferable when making your selection at this time. Totally unrealistic goals lead only to frustration, and perhaps burnout.

Making these lists is an important part of the process, according to McCallum. "By writing these items down, you are clearly telling yourself what is acceptable to you today in terms of goals and what is not acceptable." McCallum adds, "You see, what all of us have—right now—is the sum total of our goals up until this point. This includes the amount of money we are making, the degree of success we are allowing, and the extent to which we are fulfilled and happy." Since these old goals are well entrenched, it's important to communicate the new ones as clearly as possible to your subconscious.

Now, on another sheet of paper, list the components of your ideal career or work situation. Suppose you could have the ideal situation. What would it look like? In making this list, suspend disbelief, pull out all the stops, and fantasize your ideal career or work situation.

Remember that you don't have to know, and probably won't know, how you will achieve this ideal state. It doesn't matter. The process works even if you don't understand how it works.

At the top of this list, write "My ideal career/work situation allows me to . . ." and state each item in the present tense, being as specific as possible (such as "travel up to one week a month; meet my quotas easily and successfully; work flexible hours of my choosing; work in a stimulating, pleasant environment; earn $60,000 per year").

Additionally, suggests McCallum, you may want to consider the quality of your business relationships, where you want to work, how much vacation time you desire, what you wear to work, and how much supervision you would like.

In this process, you can tap the creativity of your right brain by stimulating it through the use of colored pens, pictures, and symbols. Try indicating travel by drawing rough pictures of airplanes or cars, perhaps draw smiling faces to signify your wish for a pleasant environment. Generally, use symbols or pictures instead of words wherever you can.

If you're afraid that being specific about the money you want may limit you, simply add two words to the opening sentence so that it reads: "My ideal career-work situation allows me to earn . . . (or better)."

Now, how can you begin planning ways to make your goals into reality? Let's consider a few.

Using Your Imagination

One of the simplest and most effective ways to achieve your goals is to marshall the power of your imagination. Suppose your goal is to succeed at an important business meeting or event coming up. One approach is the visualization process, a technique whose success has been documented in the now classic book, *Psychocybernetics*, by Maxwell Maltz. Here's how to use the technique:

- Sit back in your chair, take a deep breath, relax, and allow your eyes to close. To help yourself relax, focus your attention on your breath, noticing how you inhale and exhale. Just take note of it, without trying to change anything about the way you are breathing.
- Now, remember how in the past you mentally called up images of scenes from favorite movies, or how your parents looked the last time you saw them. Use this same technique of visualizing to picture the meeting or event you are concerned about.
- In your imagination, see who is at this meeting. Notice what you and the others are wearing, and where the meeting is being held. Is it in your office? In a restaurant? If so, what are people eating or drinking?
- What would you like to hear people saying to you in this meeting? What would the ideal outcome be?
- Imagine people saying exactly what you would like to hear them say. Imagine representing yourself with all the confidence, poise, wisdom, information, and persuasiveness you'd like to convey.
- Use as many of your senses—sight, hearing, touch, taste, and smell—as you can to make the scene as real as possible.

Visualizations often take time to emerge and grow. Although what you visualize may seem sketchy the first few times you try, stay with it. Watch how it develops and perhaps even changes as you begin to define more clearly exactly what it is you want.

It is useful to practice visualization for short-term goals

throughout the day, especially if you find yourself worried about a particular issue. When the worry pops up, substitute your positive visualization for the negative worry.

Visualize your ideal career each morning before getting out of bed and at night just before bed. During the day, says McCallum, if you start to worry while you're busy, instead of undertaking the whole visualization, substitute a picture, and a feeling, of pure white light for the worry. This can positively redirect the negative focus of your worry.

You can use visualization for other short-term and long-term goals, including those involving money, employee relationships, proposals you have to write, family situations . . . anything you're concerned about. Just "see," "hear," and "experience" the perfect outcome in your imagination.

Ready, Fire, Aim

Reaching goals requires focusing on them and taking appropriate action. Peters and Waterman, authors of *In Search of Excellence*, observed that for too many years American businesses were stuck in the "ready, aim, fire" mode. The first step in any new project, "ready," was to gather reams of data, and then analyze, assess, and evaluate what needed to be done. Next came "aim"—careful planning, test marketing, or simulation—followed by "fire"—actually getting started on the project.

A different concept—ready, fire, aim—can readily be used in planning your career. This idea, discussed by Peters and Waterman, involves making a *brief* assessment of your skills and the career direction you anticipate, followed by an early "firing," or getting into the actual activity quickly. The "aim," which involves readjusting, modifying, or honing career plans, should be the final task.

Let's look at an example. Mark works for the human resources (what used to be called personnel) division of a large manufacturing company. He has compiled the lists discussed earlier, which pointed out graphically that to reach his financial or long-term advancement goals, he would have to move from his current job.

Mark checks the salary ranges in his company and compares the position descriptions with his skills and abilities. The best match he finds is a position with the marketing department.

Rather than evaluating any further, Mark joins the local chapter of the American Marketing Association, has lunch with three of the marketers currently in the division, and plants a bug in the ear of the vice president of marketing about wanting a career change.

Mark has now taken control of the situation and made a series of quick moves. Later, if he finds serious career disadvantages to joining the marketing department, he can re-examine his plan.

The ready, fire, aim concept helps you start full-scale activities quickly while minimizing wasted time and energy. It gives you a chance to make small mistakes in your career path and quickly retreat from them.

Establishing Milestones

Establishing milestones for the realization of the career goals you've chosen is essential. Start with a list of possible career goals. It might include goals like these:

To earn $1 million in ten years.
To be transferred to the London division of the company.
To be featured in the company newsletter.
To be mentioned in *Forbes* magazine.
To publish a book.

Chances are that no two people will have exactly the same goals. Based on your own list, prepare a milestone chart (see Figure 1–1), showing when you plan to accomplish each of your

Figure 1–1. Milestone chart.

Goal	Year One	Year Two	Year Three
Meet five marketing directors	───		
Write article	───		
Increase salary to 45K	───		
Appear on three radio talk shows		─── ───	───
Write first book		───────	
Be featured in my industry's major journal		───	───
Be promoted to assistant department manager		───	───
Attend special executive development program		───	
Increase salary to 55K			───
Write second book			───────

goals. This is an easy way to maintain command of the timing and progress toward your established goals.

Your milestone chart could delineate each goal and subgoal, including starting time, anticipated ending time, and a schedule of subgoals—you can load it up with interim dates to aid in your progress and overall planning.

Let's say, for example, that you have set the goal of making the acquaintance of five marketing directors from other companies in your field. You wish to accomplish this through attending meetings and writing letters, with follow-up telephone calls, within six months from now. On your milestone chart, you must plot this six-month period and follow through. Unlike the would-be dieter who is always going to start next week, your campaign begins the moment your milestone chart calls for commencing the activity plotted. If you want to change your milestone chart, of course, that's fine, but as prolific career development author S. Norman Fiengold says, "You can't fool life."

If the task or activity is something that you have never undertaken before, such as writing articles for exposure, obviously you must be generous in allocating time for its accomplishment. A common weakness of most capable people is to unrealistically estimate the time it will take to accomplish something. By adding a safety margin, your probability of reaching your goal is greater.

It's vital to fine-tune your goals on a regular basis. A goal you set two months or two years ago may be inappropriate today because of changes brought about by reaching other goals, changes in your home life, or changes in the external environment.

Commitment

The key to the whole concept of goal setting is commitment, without which no doors will open for you and none of life's treasure chests will be unlocked. "I think true overnight successes are extremely rare," states noted author Herman Holtz. "Successes may come suddenly and swiftly, after a lengthy struggle, but that lengthy struggle is almost always the prior necessity." Once you've chosen your goals and established some milestones, you owe it to yourself to make the effort. It doesn't do much good to build yourself up by listing, visualizing, and preparing goals without fully dedicating yourself to achieving them.

Setting career goals will not guarantee success, but evidence strongly supports the theory that goal attainment is far more likely if those goals are clearly identified and serve as a focus.

Goal setting is the first and most important step you can take on your career marketing path. The following chapters introduce and discuss various strategies, techniques, and tools to market your career and help you attain your goals.

Chapter 2

Time Management and Career Marketing

Priorities are easy. "Posteriorities"—what jobs not to tackle—are tough.

Peter Drucker

Over the years, I've spoken to hundreds of groups and thousands of individuals on career marketing. Many are motivated to achieve their goals and a large number already possess the requisite skills. However, the one thing everyone seems to say that they don't have enough of is time. Write a press release? Prepare a speech? Who's got time? Perhaps there is no greater obstacle to effective career marketing than managing one's time.

13

Is there enough time to do your job, market your career, and otherwise lead a balanced life? Yes, there is. This chapter addresses fundamental—and not so fundamental—aspects of time management so that you will be able to do your job and be able to act on the advice in succeeding chapters to market your career.

Making Work Count Twice

The time you have available must be spread over what could be an endless number of choices. Time spent among the general areas—work, family, play, and yourself—should be balanced. But, how can you manage your time when faced with increasing demands in all areas?

Early in my career I hit upon the notion of making my work count twice. For example, at the end of each consulting engagement I had to prepare a report. From many reports I was able to extract passages that could be converted into articles that were later published. Many of those articles were used once again in books as chapters or parts of chapters, such as this one.

The same technique can be applied to other kinds of work. The key is: after completing any task, ask yourself whether the results can be used in any other way—to solve a different problem, meet someone else's need, or create a new and profitable line of business. Once you get into the habit of thinking in this way, you'll be surprised at how effective it can be.

Avoiding Time Wasters

Recognizing where your time is wasted is another way to give yourself more time for career marketing. If you do too many simple tasks yourself rather than delegating them to your subordinates, the obvious solution is to delegate more. Keep track of your time, in 15-minute intervals, if necessary, to judge where your time is spent. A list of guidelines to help you manage telephone time, such as the example in Figure 2–1 later in this chapter, can be modified for meetings or any other of your activities.

Another excellent way to make time for things you consider important is to learn to say "no!" How many of us end up doing things we feel only mild about because we haven't learned to say the word "no"? That word, which must be practiced, should be couched in something positive. If someone asks you to review a paper, for instance, say "I'd really like to, but I'm pressed for time right now so I'll have to pass."

Be ruthless in avoiding time wasters and stick to your plan of target dates and priorities. Select your priorities carefully. Make sure you do not let anything interfere with your plans for a certain segment of time.

Be particularly careful with your time when you are "on a roll." Don't let anything interrupt you if you are really producing. Lock the door, unplug the phone, do whatever it takes to maintain the momentum. Tape record meetings if you can't take notes fast enough. Also, invest in time-saving devices. Any piece of equipment that pays for itself in a year is worth it. My friend Bill let years pass without plunking down $200 to secure an item that would double his productivity. He felt "the company should pay for it." What a career loss!

Using Travel Time

The average American commutes 157,589 miles to work during his or her lifetime, the equivalent of traveling six times around the world. Think of the staggering proportion of commuting time that you spend sitting in traffic jams—and then plan some ways of using that time productively.

Install a cassette player in your car. Tapes are now available for such items as management and business books, classic novels, and old radio shows. Slip some extra reading material into your car also. Those minutes and hours spent sitting in unavoidable traffic *can* be used wisely.

If you travel by air to any of the hub cities, such as New York, Chicago, or Atlanta, you will almost surely spend some time you didn't anticipate on the runway or in the terminal. Similar to installing a cassette player and carrying extra reading material in your car for everyday use, you should always be prepared while you are traveling. Bring the stack of items you've wanted to get to, read them, and mail the package back to yourself. Maybe you won't get to use the time, but there is nothing so frustrating as not having anything to do.

ORGANIZATION—THE TIME-SAVING KEY

There is no question that getting organized and staying that way takes time and thought, but it saves even more time than it takes and yields peace of mind in addition. It's time to view getting organized as preparation time "to respond to life." Knowing where things are—papers you need for a report, back-up supplies, important phone numbers and addresses—gives you the freedom to concentrate on creative, fulfilling work.

Save time by making up address labels for people to whom you write frequently. Use return addresses as labels for your next correspondence with that person. Think of the time you spend running to the post office because you used the 20 stamps you bought last week. Buy a roll of 100 stamps at a time; you will most likely need them. The same advice holds true for any supply you use.

Getting Organized

Organization is individual, uniquely you. A desk or office that would drive you crazy may be perfectly organized for a co-worker. Keeping yourself comfortably organized will reduce your stress, increase your productivity, and influence others to view you as a competent professional.

Establish your files in advance. Having the items you need on hand will lower your frustration level.

Getting organized affords a sense of being in control of your life, rather than having your life control you. This sense of well-being will spread into other areas of your life.

Why is the perception that you are organized important in your career marketing effort? Organized people are viewed, wrongly or rightly, as more capable than disorganized persons. The impression you create by being in control adds points in your favor.

How Organized Are You?

1. Is your desk at work or at home piled horizontally with reports, papers, and notebooks? No one can manage a horizontal pile.
2. Do you have trouble finding a particular item in your desk that you use frequently? Maybe it should be left *on* your desk.
3. Do you feel that you could be organized if you only had more space? More space is seldom the answer; filing or getting rid of what isn't important is.
4. Do you have piles of newspapers and magazines at home that you don't have time to read? If you're attempting to read these publications cover to cover, good luck. Clip out what looks important or interesting, and chuck the rest.
5. Are there papers on your desk that have been there for at least a week? A desk is not a filing cabinet.
6. Do you ever find something at the bottom of a pile that you didn't know was there? This is a danger sign because you're liable to lose anything! Break down your piles now.
7. Do you sometimes spend five to ten minutes or more looking for a letter or document that you need? The search should take no more than 45 to 75 seconds. More than that and, well . . . you're wasting everyone's time.

8. Do you read every piece of unsolicited or junk mail that crosses your desk? Most of this mail can be discarded at once. Take just a few seconds to determine whether to keep, route, or throw out junk mail.

Getting the Most Out of Calls

By using the charts in Figure 2–1, adapted from those developed by management consultants David and Ann Murphy Springer, you can identify telephone time thieves. Simply log every incoming and outgoing call for two weeks or until you feel you have mastered "the beast."

Your Productivity Cycle

Most people have productive peaks and valleys throughout the course of the normal work week—periods of higher and lower energy and creativity. This pattern makes up your own *cycle of productivity*. For all but urgent assignments, you should try to handle assignments on those days and at those hours that achieve a relatively constant "effort-to-task" ratio.

Productive people who are able to pace themselves can accomplish more in less time and remain more vibrant. They have an internal "time grid" that charts their cycle of productivity, even though no formal sketch or chart is ever made. Don't be leery of telling your supervisor that you'd "rather not handle the DEF report right now" because you "can do a better job on it tomorrow morning," and the "GHI assignment could be better undertaken now." If neither report represents an emergency, your schedule should prevail.

Given that you're already a highly productive employee, there are four basic ways to get the most from yourself by working in sync with your cycle of productivity.

Figure 2–1. Identifying telephone time thieves.

Telephone Time Manager—Outgoing Calls

To _____ Date _____

Is this call necessary? _____
What priority is it? _____
Is agenda prepared? _____
Are notes, info at hand? _____
Is this the right time to call? _____
Can other issues be dealt with? _____
Were chatting, wandering minimized? _____
Was the issue resolved? _____
Person was unavailable/no answer/I left message _____
Recipient didn't have info _____
I was redirected to another person _____
Further action needed _____

Target Time _____
Actual Time _____

Telephone Time Manager—Incoming Calls

From _____ Date _____

Is this call necessary? _____
Could someone else have effectively dealt with the caller? _____
Was a subordinate asking for info that he or she could have gotten
   otherwise? _____
Was I able to help the caller? _____
Did I get the info I wanted? _____
Was the issue resolved? _____
Was a decision made? _____
Do I know what further action I need to take? _____
Did I minimize chatting, wandering? _____

Target Time _____
Actual Time _____

1. Ask for enough assignments so that the cycle can be used. If you have only one task, obviously, there is little leeway in undertaking that task at the most personally opportune time. With numerous assignments, however, you can strategically arrange your schedule.

2. Seek flexibility in due dates. You know you'll productively finish the important jobs on time. Assignments of lesser importance can be finished as soon as possible. The more flexibility you are afforded in completing assignments, the greater the opportunity for you to execute assignments in accordance with the cycle. So, next time you're assigned a particular project, find out when it must be done or if it would be done following something else. More often than not, given a flexible due date, you will complete many assignments sooner than you anticipated.

3. Work with your boss to avoid late afternoon and surprise assignments. As a productive employee, in concurrence with your cycle of productivity, you intuitively allocate tasks for the late afternoon. Frequent late afternoon surprise assignments mess up your cycle.

4. Closely related to the above, always try to obtain advance notice of assignments. The more notice you have, the better you'll be able to schedule the new assignment in accordance with your cycle of productivity.

"CONCENTRATED" CAREER MARKETING

Concentration is the ability to focus attention voluntarily, to ignore irrelevant proceedings, and to fix power and effort to a single goal. Concentration is a time management tool that can be increased through practice.

Common distractions abound. If you are looking for a reason not to get a job done or not to concentrate on a task, plenty exist. In fact, anything can become a distraction to your concentration if you allow it to happen. Distractions dissipate your energy level and reduce your productivity with a resulting increase in your level of stress.

The first step, then, in increasing your power of concentration is to eliminate outside distractions! Taking control of your life in this way will increase your confidence and enhance your career marketing efforts. You are in charge, not those who call you on the telephone or otherwise fritter away your time.

Hold telephone calls.

To the degree that you can, hold calls and post signs on your office door. One association executive was so bothered with constant phone calls that he instructed his secretary to tell all callers that he would take calls only between 3 and 5 P.M. This was the time of day that he felt least able to concentrate on planning and oversight duties, and most comfortable talking to people.

Within three weeks, his phone never rang before three o'clock in the afternoon. People calling in didn't mind; they just readjusted their schedules to accommodate his. If you think about it, probably 90 percent of all your phone calls can wait for a few hours. As long as you have some time each day set aside for answering telephone calls, you will be aware enough of any emergency.

Another advantage to answering telephone calls later is that you have time to arrange the information you may need for the call (see Figure 2–1 again). Have the appropriate folder on your desk when you return a call.

Use transition time.

Transition time, the five minutes it takes you to walk to your office or the twenty-five minutes to drive to work or the hour on the commuter train, can be used to increase your concentration. This time, so often spent daydreaming or worrying, can be used to focus your attention in an orderly way on the meeting or task to come. If you anticipate a rough meeting, there is no need to become frantic. Just think about the upcoming chore, put it into an overall perspective, and acknowledge its importance to your plan of action.

Visually say no to distractions.

If you find yourself having trouble saying no to unwanted social obligations or business commitments that distract you from your major goals, create a mental picture of yourself overcoming the distraction.

Poet Elisavietta Ritchie puts the word *no* on her telephone and at the desk where she answers her mail, to help her turn down speaking engagements and requests for writing advice that become destructive to her own time.

Avoid watching the clock.

Use an alarm clock rather than a watch or clock to keep track of time. The temptation to look at the time every five minutes is greater than most of us can resist. An alarm clock with its face hidden, across the room or even tucked into a drawer, will alert you when it's time to move on to another task or to end your day.

Make promises to yourself.

If you absolutely cannot bring your attention back to a task, try an overnight focus. Let it go for that day, but promise yourself to come to it with a new focus the next morning.

Challenge yourself.

If a task is boring, making it difficult to concentrate, turn it into a challenge. How many envelopes can you seal in ten minutes? How many different ways can you discover to stuff a packet full of 15 different pieces of information? Such techniques will make the time go much faster.

CREATIVITY AND TIME MANAGEMENT

What does nurturing your creativity have to do with time management? Plenty! Creativity is represented by novel approaches to problems and issues. People who follow the same routine day in and day out are very likely to be wasting large chunks of time.

Use of creative approaches to the tasks at hand leads to new time-saving breakthroughs and possibilities whether in your job or in your career marketing program. The following are just a few factors that can increase your creativity *and* save time.

Check the weather forecast.

Many people do some of their best creative thinking when the weather is overcast. The reasons for this aren't exactly clear, but perhaps a nice day filled with bright sunshine stymies the creative thinking process—or just makes you want to be outside! Although you can't schedule a rainy day in advance, it does make good sense to take advantage of what nature has to offer. If you're one of those people who do think creatively when the weather outside is frightful, why not "go with the flow." Look over the long-term plan that's been sitting in your upper drawer for the past several weeks. Or arrange a brainstorming session with co-workers to overcome current problems.

Check the clock.

Most individuals find that they do their best creative thinking early in the morning, although a significant number find their peak period to be midmorning or late at night. A far lesser number find their most creative time in the evening; less than one in 12 judge themselves most creative during the afternoon.

If you're not sure what time of day you are at your creative best, monitor yourself over a one- or two-week period. This can be done by keeping a time log of what activities you undertake and when—sort of similar to checking your productivity cycle— and also by noting your energy level and enthusiasm throughout the various parts of each day.

As a result of keeping this log, you may be surprised to find that you should perhaps perform analysis, write reports, or undertake professional reading at a different schedule than you've been doing.

Consider what helps.

Other factors that may be conducive to your personal creativity include, but are not limited to, wearing comfortable clothes, having extra space on your immediate desk, using your favorite writing instrument, or changing your physical posture (walking, pacing, standing).

Also, you might try readjusting the height of your seat, or experimenting with the type, size, and color of paper you use to write on.

Consider what hinders.

It's quite possible that factors that hinder concentration also hinder creativity, such as the ring of your phone, the color of your office walls, the presence or absence of background sounds, the sense of impending interruptions, or the feeling that just sitting and thinking does not look productive.

Certainly too little sleep or too much sleep won't help. Neither will skipping breakfast or consuming heavy breads and pastas for lunch. Researchers have found that when the digestive system has a lot of work to do, the brain is robbed of oxygen, which leads to the afterlunch blahs. The solution is to eat a light lunch and take a walk afterward. I find that scheduling too tightly stifles my creativity; I just can't think clearly when rushed. Many professionals, particularly in large corporations, find that criticism or even fear of criticism is definitely a creativity "downer."

Make big problems smaller.

Large, unsolvable problems can usually be broken into smaller, more manageable issues. "Quiet, calm deliberation disentangles every knot" is one of my favorite sayings. If a problem arises that seems unsolvable, take a few minutes to think about it quietly. Make sure you will have no distractions, close your door, put your feet on your desk, close your eyes, and take several deep breaths. This advice is repeated so often that it seems like a cliche, but *it works!*

Once you break the big problem down, list the smaller tasks in priority order, and tackle them one at a time. Let's say you have a proposal to write for your company. Breaking it into eight sections will allow you to make a checkmark next to each section as it is finished. That's eight minicelebrations, rather than just one for the whole proposal. The feeling of accomplishment at the end of each small task will create more energy and confidence for moving on to the next.

If you're similar to most professionals, you've undoubtedly experienced days and weeks on end when you hardly had a moment to spare, let alone a moment to undertake highly creative thinking toward your career marketing efforts. This is a serious mistake and one that should not continue to be given "back burner" status. Your ability to think creatively and strategically is vital to your career.

Chapter 3

Cultivating Your Professional Image

For the great majority of mankind is satisfied with appearances, as though they were realities, and is more often influenced by the things that seem than by those that are.

Machiavelli

One of the first people I asked for advice when I decided to "go for it" as a sought-after author was a wardrobe consultant. Judy Brannock offered courses through a local adult education program on shaping your image through wardrobe. I hired her expressly for the purpose of coming to look at my closet.

On our first meeting, I opened up my closet doors. I was aware that several of my shirts were old, the collars frayed, and perhaps some of them didn't go with my coloring. Nevertheless, I was sure that at least one-half to one-third were salvageable. I thought I would round out my wardrobe by purchasing new ones as she recommended.

Less than thirty seconds after I opened the closet doors, she said in a clear, authoritative tone, "Throw them all out."

I was aghast! *"All* of them?" I asked.

Judy turned toward me and slowly and carefully said, "Read my lips—all of them."

For the balance of the afternoon, we discussed what I would need to buy, including what color, what material, and from which stores. Judy also looked at my ties (largely polyester) and told me to replace them all with silk. She looked at my shoes, she looked at my suits, she looked at my belts, and she looked at my overcoat.

From top to bottom, it was clear. What I wanted to be and what I was projecting were not in sync. It was of no value to my overall goals to continue to wear what I was wearing because my clothes were functional, when New York publishers and others whom I wanted to influence needed to feel "right" about me in their own ways. The only way to ensure that those publishers and others would feel "right," at least from a wardrobe standpoint, was to be impeccably dressed.

After a lot of moaning and groaning in the weeks that followed, I replaced my entire wardrobe, offering the remains to the Salvation Army and Goodwill Industries. Looking back, the whole process should have been simple, but oh, the things that get in our way before we finally make the correct decisions.

My goal of becoming a sought-after author was much more important to me than the lesser, never-stated goal of continuing to get as much use out of my clothing as humanly possible, and so my image had to change.

Why Image Counts

Communication experts and social scientists believe that what you look like—your overall appearance, facial expressions, age, gender, and body language—compose a good part of the total message you present to another person at your first meeting.

Think of your own first impressions of others. What do you usually notice first about a person? How does what you first notice affect the relationship later? Would you listen more carefully to a man in a green leisure outfit or to a man in a gray, three-piece business suit? Would a woman who couldn't meet your eyes make you feel comfortable about buying the product she is selling?

The problem with making a bad first impression or presenting a continuing negative image is that the words you use won't matter. Communication, so vital to career advancement, simply will not take place. The other person won't be paying attention.

To advance your career, you need an image that enhances or complements the image that your company presents to clients. Does your firm present itself as dynamic, up-to-date, vibrant? If so, your own image should reflect those qualities. In that case, you would probably wear brighter clothes and project a higher energy level than someone looking to advance in a conservative company priding itself on stability.

Knowing what image you present is more difficult than it would seem at first glance. Perceiving yourself exactly as others do is impossible. However, you can check your perceptions with those of a coworker or friend and combine that information with your own.

A Common Misconception

The statement "I want to be promoted on the basis of my performance and not the way I present myself" typifies a common misconception of how the world works. People have nothing to go on when they first meet you *except* the way you look and act. The first impression is usually lasting, largely because peoples' perceptions are not easily changed, but also because you are likely to keep projecting the same image.

The way you look and what that conveys are part of your performance. Recognize that the way you look affects the way you work and the way other people perceive your work. Cultivating your image means defining and focusing more sharply on who you really are. "It is of the utmost importance that you be authentic and genuine and that you not seek artificially to blot out aspects of who you are and the way you act," says Dr. Jeffrey Lant in his book *The Unabashed Self-Promoter.*

Your image can make it easy for others to understand and identify with you. If you know that the group you will be with is dressing very casually, wear a flannel shirt and blue jeans. You would make the members and yourself uncomfortable by wearing a business suit.

Factors that Affect Image

Appearance, facial expression, personal space, and body language all affect your personal image. Give careful thought to all these factors. (Note the checklist in Figure 3–1 on pages 34–35.)

Appearance.

Clothing, hairstyle, and accessories are important elements of how you appear to others. Dark colors are still preferred in professional clothing, especially for men. If you are a woman, and the powerful women in your firm always wear suits, take your cue from them and avoid wearing dresses or slacks. Jewelry should be simple, preferably gold, and never loud. Your hair should be short to mid-length and neat. Fingernails should look manicured for both men and women.

Even if red spiked heels are all the rage in Paris and New

York, wear yours to social events, not to the office. Men should also pay close attention to such parts of the wardrobe as shoes and ties. Understated clothes are generally safe in almost any office situation. Dress to blend in with the other professionals in your setting. Let your work stand out, not your fashions.

Facial expressions.

A broad, friendly smile puts across an image of trust that will serve you well. In addition to smiling, look the other person directly in the eyes.

Train yourself to become aware of how the facial expressions of others affect your own behavior. Does a coworker's smile that lasts just a bit too long make you uncomfortable, make him seem perhaps untrustworthy? Does a client's open smile allow you to feel comfortable around her? Once you heighten your awareness of this factor, among others we discuss, you will be better able to judge how your own mannerisms and appearance affect others—the first step to altering your image.

Personal space.

The amount of space with which a person feels comfortable around him- or herself depends on the person and the situation. Standing too close to someone generally means that you feel you have more power than the other person does. It usually makes people uncomfortable and should be used only when you need to assert yourself. On the other hand, a person who continually backs away may seem afraid or untrustworthy.

Judge the space with which another person feels comfortable rather than your own distance. Al, who had been a minister, felt comfortable standing close to people. He did not stand close as a power play, but because of the nature of his former profession. However, standing close was inappropriate in the sales field, and Al continually had problems with clients.

Experiment with personal space variables to see where you feel most comfortable and how your distance from others makes them feel.

Body language.

Your posture and bearing tell others how you feel about yourself. And that tells your supervisors if you are able to advance. An erect, relaxed bearing promises confidence and competence.

Watch out for nervous habits. Although you may not even be aware that you are drumming your fingers on the desk or pushing back your fingernail cuticles, such actions are a dead giveaway to nervousness or a lack of confidence.

Other important factors.

Skin color, gender, and age are also important factors of your image. Although you can't change them, you can recognize their effect and plan around it. Janet Elsea, author of *First Impression, Best Impression,* believes that skin color still "remains the most dominant characteristic of physical appearance in this society."

She points out that skin color is an important factor if your color does not meet the expectations of the people with whom you are working. "Initially, seek to counter stereotypes by paying extra attention to your appearance, facial expressions, eye contact and other physical attributes," advises Elsea.

As more minorities advance in business fields, the importance of skin color as a first impression factor should decrease. And as more women advance in business fields, the importance of gender as a factor in image should decrease. However, being a woman, especially in the upper management roles, still means running into obstacles that are not there for most males. Use the prevailing perception of a woman in upper management as a trendsetter to your advantage by linking it to your willingness to forge ahead and to take chances, when necessary, for the business.

If you are young, you may be seen as brash or inexperienced. An older person, however, may be perceived as worn out or too conservative and settled to create any new ideas. Younger workers should stress their past successes; older people could emphasize their fresh approaches to problem-solving. Counterbalance the possible negative images that your age may convey by stressing the positive ones.

Your voice is an important factor in your image. Voice characteristics include speed, loudness, pitch, tone, and articulation.

Elsea recommends taping yourself, either in conversation or reading aloud, the first thing in the morning (when you're most relaxed and fresh), in the early afternoon (when stress and exhaustion tend to be high), and late evening (when you are relaxed but tired). Through the tapes, you may discover one or more of these typical problems:

- Monotony, a lack of variation in pitch levels, may be interpreted as a lack of caring or boredom.
- A rising or upward inflection at the end of sentences gives the impression of tentativeness.
- Talking through your nose is distracting to listeners. (To find out if you are a nasal speaker, Elsea recommends pinching your nose closed and saying aloud, "Whoa, oh horse of mine." There should be no vibrations in your nose except for the word *mine*.) To correct this problem, open your mouth more and try speaking more loudly.
- Stridency, or a shrill voice, conveys extreme nervousness. This is caused by insufficient breathing. Relaxation exercises, such as yawning, rolling your neck, and massaging your jaw, can help relieve this problem.

Some voice problems require drastic correction. Martha was the vice president of marketing for a large architectural firm, but her high and squeaky voice made her sound childish. Clients were always remarking that her voice did not fit her level of competence. She is currently taking speech lessons to lower her pitch.

The image factors covered in this chapter are only a few of those that make up this important career marketing "tool" we call "image." To help analyze the factors your image comprises, use the chart in Figure 3–1. It will also help you to decide how you can best change your image to your benefit.

If your image is not helping you to advance in your career, you need to change it. This is likely to take time since long-developed behaviors are hard to alter.

Figure 3–1. Checking your image.

Make three blank copies of this list. On one copy, describe the way you present yourself for each of the categories. For instance, under the category "shoes," you might describe your typical shoes as "black or brown, slightly worn heels with scuff marks on top." Or under the category "posture, bearing," you might describe your normal posture as "erect but not rigid." Then list what you think that conveys to other people. Using the "shoe" example, you may write that your typical shoes convey a careless attitude.

After you have filled out the form yourself, give one copy to a coworker you trust and the other copy to your spouse or a close friend. Ask them to write the same information about you. Use parts of each of the three perceptions to analyze your image.

	Description of my usual . . .	What that conveys . . .
Personal Appearance		
Wardrobe:		
suit	_____	_____
shirts/blouses	_____	_____
ties/scarves	_____	_____
shoes	_____	_____
belts	_____	_____
coats	_____	_____
glasses	_____	_____
jewelry	_____	_____
briefcase	_____	_____
Personal:		
hair style	_____	_____
fingernails	_____	_____
beard or moustache	_____	_____
makeup	_____	_____
eyebrows	_____	_____

Figure 3–1, continued

	Description of my usual . . .	What that conveys . . .
Body Language		
Physical characteristics:		
posture/bearing	_____	_____
facial expressions	_____	_____
nervous habits	_____	_____
hand gestures	_____	_____
eye contact	_____	_____
personal space	_____	_____
touch	_____	_____
Voice characteristics:		
rate of speech	_____	_____
volume of speech	_____	_____
pitch (monotonous or singsong)	_____	_____
nasality	_____	_____
resonance	_____	_____
Atmospherics		
Automobile:		
year, make	_____	_____
exterior condition	_____	_____
interior condition	_____	_____
Office:		
decor/pictures	_____	_____
desktop cleanliness	_____	_____
Accessories:		
type of pen	_____	_____
purse/wallet	_____	_____
business cards	_____	_____
cigarettes/cigars	_____	_____

Chapter 4

Finding a Career Counselor or Mentor

Two are better than one; for if they fall, the one will lift up his fellow; but woe to him that is alone when he falleth, and hath not another to lift him up.

Ecclesiastes

You may have noted that the title of Part I is You Are Your Own Career Coach, yet this chapter obviously concerns finding a career counselor or mentor. An obvious contradiction?

Not really. Wherever you go, whatever you do in your career, you can be sure that *you* are the only one who will be there every step of the way. You will be making an endless number of decisions on your own. But at any point along the journey, if you can get competent help, it pays to use it. Peers, parents, mentors all may help. If you find a good career counselor, only a few hours a month will keep you focused on your goals and moving steadily toward them.

SELECTING A CAREER COUNSELOR

Before selecting a career counselor, you might want to ask yourself if such a person would be worthwhile. Psychologist Harry A. Olson, a specialist in teaching high performance skills to business executives and sales representatives, observes that most professional and Olympic athletes have personal coaches to help them cope with competition and perform to their maximum potential. In fact, the better such athletes become, the more elite their status, and the more they need and rely on their coaches. Why? Because the higher they rise in their fields, the more critical their moves become. And the more important personal feedback becomes in avoiding mistakes. The bottom line: the coach gives them the competitive edge!

Much like sports, business is becoming more competitive every day. In response to this increase in competition, many businesses are adapting and changing; some are being drastically overhauled. This breeds new insecurity and change. The career-conscious business person must strategize more carefully and effectively than ever before to ensure his or her future and to maximize new opportunities. Also, technology in some fields is advancing faster than our ability to keep up with it. This has led to an increasingly rapid change in the quality and nature of personal demands on people's values and emotions, as well as on their time and activities.

Enter the "career coach." Olson says that such a person can help "diagnose and sort out your situation and opportunities, offer new strategies for coping with office politics and competition from other firms, and help you with and show you vital stress management skills. A good career coach helps you discover and capitalize on new opportunities, provides new tools to improve communication, and helps chart your goals and career path." Your career counselor is your personal, behind-the-scenes coach— a confidant, consultant, and resource.

Crutch or Tool?

"We don't question the wisdom of using tools to fix our cars or build wood projects, yet so often we balk at using all the resources available to build our careers," says Olson.

Many achievers value "doing it on my own." They see using "professional help" as a weakness, as if they are dependent on the helper, as if using a personal consultant or counselor somehow takes something away from themselves. Far from it. In reality, everything you do you are doing on your own because it is you who are doing it. The career counselor works behind the scenes, helping you so that you do it better.

Since 1984, I have used the career coaching services of Penny Garner, president of Taking Charge!, based in Alexandria, Virginia. We meet for only a short period each time, but I leave supercharged!

You have to remember that self-analysis is always limited, and always somewhat faulty because of self-protective "blind spots." A counselor increases your objectivity. Also, because of his or her background and training, a counselor can address a broader range of personal and career issues than you could. The counselor's primary role, says Olson, is to be a trainer, a listener, an observer, a motivator, and a sounding board.

A good counselor will help you discover your mission, assist you in mapping out your goals and strategies, and will monitor your progress. You will get objective, honest feedback on an adult-to-adult basis without moral judgments. The counselor will neither command you to do something nor let you flounder. He or she will help you sort out options clearly and objectively. The ultimate decisions and actions are always your own.

Your goals and needs are always the specific foundation of your relationship with the counselor. A career counselor is committed to doing everything in his or her power to help you meet those objectives. As an objective observer, he or she can help you sort through complex situations and help you determine your best strategies.

In the last analysis, you alone must decide if a career counselor is for you. However, says Olson, if you experience or are faced with any of the following, the answer is probably yes:

1. Organizational changes within your company, especially if they have a direct impact on you.
2. Acquisitions or mergers.
3. Expansion into new markets.
4. Diversification into new products or services.
5. Increased competition to your company from other firms trying to take over your market share.
6. Increased management or supervisory responsibility.
7. Increased leadership opportunities.
8. A recent or soon-to-be-available promotion.
9. A new boss or leadership shake-up above you.
10. Changes in your role or assignments within your company.
11. In-company competition and power plays, corporate intrigue, jockeying for position, turf protection—especially if you're on the rise, because the higher you go, often the worse it gets.
12. Blockades of your progress by internal feuds or informal political processes.
13. Excess stress on the job.
14. Increased media exposure and/or public speaking requirements.
15. Increased production or sales quotas.

16. A new project you must lead or participate in developing.
17. Quality Circles or Intrapreneuring groups.
18. Being a woman, black or Hispanic, or any other ethnic or racial minority, or being disabled.
19. A strong desire to advance in your company or profession, regardless of whether you experience any of the above.

How and Whom to Choose

If by now you're convinced that it makes sense to hire a career counselor, there are several steps to choosing the right one.

First, determine your needs. Once you've determined them, you can direct the counselor as to how he or she can help you most. Your counselor can also help you define your needs more explicitly.

The next step is to find the counselor. The best way to begin is to seek referrals or try the Yellow Pages under various headings such as "Counselors," "Advisors," or "Consultants." Olson recommends asking a lot of questions when you do identify some career counselors. Most professionals today are used to being questioned by prospective clients.

1. Ask about training. What was his or her specialty? Ask about the business-relatedness of the specialty if this is not apparent.
2. Find out about experience related to coaching business people, and also ask about experience working with high performance methods and motivation techniques. Has the person had any direct coaching experience whether in sports, music, drama, or speaking? Remember that the average counselor is not trained in coaching skills. These are picked up along the way.
3. Check fee and payment arrangements. Most counselors will

quote an hourly figure, although some may work with you on a retainer basis.

4. If you feel that the person is probably not right for you, ask for a referral or two to other professionals so that you can check out other options before making a decision. Such a request will not offend the counselor.

The concept of a career counselor is viewed by some as revolutionary. Yet serious, career-minded professionals at the cutting edge of their professions are availing themselves of this opportunity more and more every day.

THE MENTOR-PROTÉGÉ CONNECTION

The word *mentor* brings to mind a picture of a gray-haired senior executive with wisdom and experience to share with the eager junior executive. However, of the five mentors I have been fortunate enough to have had in the past ten years, only one was a senior executive at an organization where I was employed. One mentor is a man closer to my age with whom I have almost a "co-mentor" relationship. I also have a mentor I've met only once—a luminary in the field of marketing with whom I communicate mainly by mail. It's also possible to have a mentor who does not give advice, but from whom you learn simply by example. Yet, notwithstanding the possible varieties of mentor-protégé relationships, there are several denominators common to all.

Typical Features

A mentor gives you *support* within the corporate world. If you are new to the business climate, it can seem full of rules and nuances that weren't taught in college. A mentor will guide you through the learning process, giving you clues to the subtleties of the workplace.

For instance, Bob takes his protégé, Tom, and a senior colleague, who is knowledgeable about company politics, out to lunch. Tom sits quietly, listening to the gossip and picking up on skills, such as how to handle the check and how deferential or friendly to be to an executive of the company.

Knowledge and skills acquisition is another important part of the mentor-protégé relationship. It becomes an accelerated learning process for you. A mentor may read over your reports and give you feedback, take you to seminars, or discuss your work regularly.

An associate tells of her mentor, Woody. "He was both a mentor and boss to me when I was just out of college. I wanted to be a writer but worked as a secretary. Woody set aside two hours every Wednesday afternoon to 'chat.' He told me stories of his days at the *Buffalo Evening News*. We would talk about news events or the internal politics of our organization.

"The sessions were a formal way of reserving time for us when work, per se, didn't interfere," she said. Ten years later, their relationship is still strong. She sends him clips of her articles, and he sends her proofs of his books.

Yet, a mentor is usually not your boss. Having a mentor outside your company or your division is probably better in the long run. However, always be wary of a potential problem this may cause with your own boss, especially if he or she feels threatened by someone else giving you advice.

Broadened horizons are often available to you through your mentor. He or she will be pleased to introduce you to associates garnered over the years. When your mentor introduces you to important and interesting people, recognize that these are individuals it may have taken you years to meet on your own.

However, the mentor-protégé relationship is not a one-way street. The benefits to the mentor include:

- The personal satisfaction that comes with sharing knowledge and experience.
- The feeling that his or her work will live on.
- The boost to the ego that the mentor's knowledge is wanted (especially important as people get older and question their usefulness).
- The excitement, added energy, and rejuvenation of spirit that come from sharing new ideas.
- The chance to reflect on his or her experiences.

The company also benefits by receiving training for its new or junior staff from experienced people.

This system has so many benefits that it has even been formalized. The Small Business Administration has a program called SCORE (Service Corps of Retired Executives). Meetings are set up between retired business executives and people who are just starting their own businesses. The retired executives offer advice free of charge until the business owners no longer need or seek help.

Disadvantages to Both Parties

All is not rosy in the mentor-protégé relationship. There are some pitfalls to avoid. A common example is the junior who repeats the faults and weaknesses of the mentor. Emulating someone is helpful; blindly following someone is not.

Theodore J. Halatin of Southwest Texas State University warns of other possible drawbacks of the mentor-protégé relationship. These dangers are minor compared to the advantages, but you should be aware of them in order to avoid them.

- The mentor may postpone or delegate many tasks and put in much longer hours because being a mentor takes time.

- A business or social failure by one person could embarrass the other.
- Each person risks getting involved in the other's career battles (in which neither one belongs) because of the emotional tie that develops.
- Confidences exchanged during the relationship can leave one or both sides vulnerable if a rift later occurs.
- Emotional dependency can grow on either side.
- Rivals of the protégé who feel at a disadvantage can, out of jealousy, maneuver to hamper the protégé's career.

Some protégés also develop accelerated expectations. Your mentor makes it look so easy; he or she just calls someone on the phone and lands a $500,000 contract. But be comforted by the realization that it took your mentor some 25 years of experience and networking to be able to do just that.

A survey undertaken by Srully Blotnick, author of *Corporate Steeplechase*, sheds a revealing light on this subject. Blotnick followed 3,000 mentor-protégé relationships over a period of 25 years. In more than 2,000 cases, the protégé's personal growth and self-confidence were inhibited. Only 34 relationships lasted more than three years. Of the cases in which the mentor was the immediate supervisor to the protégé, 40 percent ended with the firing of the protégé.

Obviously these results call for a different approach to mentoring. "We've got to understand that mentoring is much more than just one relationship," states Boston University Professor of Organizational Behavior, Kathy Kram. "It is a system of relationships that provide support."

Where to Find a Mentor

The best approach to mentor-protégé relationships seems to be to seek as much help and advice available from as many qualified sources as possible. If a mutually satisfactory relationship can be established with just one senior executive, that is certainly fine. However, don't isolate your efforts to finding just one mentor. Rather, open your mind to your environment and absorb as much information and experience as comes your way.

The best possible mentor is an executive retired from your company. He or she is outside the mainstream of office politics, yet can chronicle the events leading to the current political situation. A retired mentor will have more time, and, therefore, be more likely to teach, as well as do favors for you.

Part **II**_____

Career Marketing on the Job

Chapter 5

Learning the Ropes

You can observe a lot by just watching.

Yogi Berra

Every company is different, not only in the products or services it provides, but in many other, more subtle ways. At XYZ Video Productions, the attitude to have is an aggressive "go-grab-the-world" one. If you're at DEF Manufacturing down the street, a quietly professional demeanor is vital for dealing with both company insiders and clients, who have come to expect such an attitude. And at RST Bank around the corner, conservatism and caution are the watchwords, even if they mean missed opportunities for business.

Knowing what makes your organization tick is important in

49

your career marketing efforts, at least for the short term. Realistically assessing your company's policies and procedures, and the underlying rationale for them, will enable you to know how best to get ahead in the atmosphere that prevails.

On my first job, as a marketing representative for a *Fortune* 500 computer manufacturer, I soon learned that the way to impress the boss the fastest was: (1) make quota (obviously), and (2) spend as little time in the office as possible. The prevailing climate at our branch office was "if you're in the office, you can't be out selling." (Never mind that the more you sold, the more paperwork you had.)

In other organizations, similar types of unwritten rules prevail. In the federal government, unfortunately, the prevailing rule tends to be "don't show too much enthusiasm for your work." My ten years in the metro Washington, D.C., area convinced me that the federal government is set up to reward mediocrity (although such may not be true in every agency or department).

Let's take a look at some of the techniques you can use to accelerate your understanding of the organization for which you work.

Orientation

Most larger companies have formal or informal orientation programs for new employees. Orientations can offer a wealth of information about your organization immediately. I've known of companies where orientation lasted one hour—just long enough for the new employee to sign W-2 forms and hear about vacation and sick leave policies. A policy manual is shoved at the new people, who are then sent to their desks. In these instances, employees learn about their company by what *is not* said at orientation.

Other companies go much further in their efforts to bring new employees on board. They spend days with a newcomer, getting that person up to speed on the organization's structure, philosophy, past experiences, and future goals. Introductions are made to all the current employees. Some companies even have video tapes that show employees and clients in action or illustrate different areas of the company.

During your orientation, ask to see copies of the office memoranda distributed in the previous two or three months. Reading these will help you assess the current work flow and political atmosphere.

Walls and Bulletin Boards

Read the walls! Your company's walls and bulletin boards are a gold mine of information about its workings. Read the plaques that appear on the lobby walls. If the plaques are awarded to company employees from outside organizations, they can tell you what other companies, agencies, or community groups are important to the image of your company. If the awards are from your company to its own employees, they will tell you the characteristics and skills valued by the company.

Bulletin boards filled with employee newsletters and suggestion boxes are usually exhibited in a company that considers the input of its employees to be important. A bulletin board with pronouncements from upper management, but no opportunity for employee input, tells a different story.

A decorating change can foretell a change in company direction. For instance, a company I worked with took down its wood panels and a wall full of awards, painted the lobby a bright pastel, and exhibited modern art—big paintings with slashes of color. It soon became obvious that this was a precursor of a change in target market from small family-owned businesses to international corporations.

The walls of individual offices in your company can be just as full of information. Check the pictures that your supervisor has hung on his or her walls. Are there patterns in the types of pictures used to decorate the offices of executives in your company as opposed to those of staff workers? Which type does your own office resemble?

Reception Rooms

Every skillful salesperson knows the discoveries available in a company's reception room. A good place to start is the magazines on the coffee tables or in the racks. The types of magazine displayed reveal something about the business. If an international travel magazine is out on view, the firm most likely takes a global approach to business. If *Forbes*, *Fortune*, or similar publications are displayed, the business is trying to project an image of sophistication and awareness of corporate life.

The receptionist can give an indication of your company's philosophy, too. Generally speaking, an older, mature receptionist may reflect management's desire to maintain an image of a well-established, reputable, traditional business, whereas a younger person in fashionable dress suggests a company that is fast-paced, energetic, and "on the move."

The setup of the reception room is another clue. A company that shields its employees from view usually has a high regard for them and is trying to convey a high class image.

Policy Manuals

New employees are often given company policy manuals when they join a firm. And, almost without fail, no one reads the manuals. Although the reading may seem dry, take the time to read through your policy manual and make notes where you don't understand or where you see opportunity.

In addition to procedural matters like regular office hours, filling out timesheets, and benefits offered, policy manuals will often include discussion of company goals, responsibilities of different positions, and promotion policies—valuable information for moving ahead.

Lunch and Social Activities

Lunches are an important part of an organization's social activities. And social activities are vital to your career advancement. Your participation in social events will increase the number of people you know in the company as well as being evidence of your ability to get along.

Use lunches as an opportunity to meet and get to know other people in your organization, especially those in divisions that complement yours or to which you might someday be interested in transferring. At the beginning of your employment, I recommend finding a soft touch in the office, a person who knows everyone and everyone's business and likes to talk. Take that person to lunch and just listen. Try, in particular, to find out the names of the hard touches, the people that office gossip says are hard to get to know. Then invite *those* people to lunch. You may be surprised at their gratitude.

Organizational Communication Patterns

We'll call him Robert Jones. He's the founder and president of a small company that produces educational video tapes. He proclaims an open door policy, encouraging his staff to come see him "any time you want." Although Jones professes an open door policy, he creates an atmosphere in company staff meetings indicating that he prefers to solve problems by himself, that outside help is really interference.

When Mary, a new employee, knocks on his door with a suggestion for a more efficient filing system, Jones thanks her and quickly ushers her out of his office. She never hears another word about her suggestion and notices that it has not been taken. Jones figuratively slammed his open door in Mary's face by not showing any interest and not providing any feedback—good or bad.

Executives often rate communications among themselves as their principal area of difficulty, as being more problematic than handling conflicts, holding better meetings, or making decisions. If corporate executives find it difficult to have probing, problem-solving conversations among themselves, imagine how much more difficult it is for them to communicate effectively with staff members throughout the company.

Although formal methods of communication, such as publishing a company newsletter or giving all employees a copy of the mission statement, are important, all too often they can be superficial attempts that push honest communication to the background. True communication, the kind that will help to maintain committed employees and probably help the profit sheet as well, is communication in which workers feel they have a stake. Face-to-face meetings are the best, since they allow the most possibilities for dialogue.

Dialogue works well at a General Motors plant in Brookhaven, Mississippi. Besides the usual communications such as a monthly newspaper, frequent meetings of employee teams, and an electronic news display in the cafeteria, management at the unionized facility holds a quarterly meeting for all employees. Plant manager J. Edward Zuga says that they discuss with employees all the relevant information on financial performance, future plans, quality performance . . . anything that might be of importance to them and the company. Such open dialogue keeps productivity high and turnover low.

Open or Closed Communication?

Ask yourself the following questions about communications in your company to determine if your firm is open or closed.

- Am I encouraged to make suggestions to my supervisors?
- Do I get feedback when I make a suggestion? Immediate feedback as well as long-term feedback?
- Does the person show a genuine interest, or seem to be pacifying me?

- Do I have a clear picture of where my company is heading and how I fit into the picture?

If your company has a pattern of open communication, take advantage of every opportunity to learn of the latest developments and to make suggestions and provide input. If the pattern is closed, outwardly trying to obtain information or attempting to provide input may get you marked as a pest. In such cases, figure out how you can be noticed without negative connotations. For instance, if direct communication is not possible, maybe the top officers get their information through reports. Who else is privy to such reports? Perhaps you could volunteer to write them. If so, make sure you are credited.

Promotion Practices

A friend I'll call Barbara French, who works for the newly titled Human Resources Division of a large telecommunications firm, said to me recently: "We used to be called the Personnel Department, but I haven't done any recruiting or outside advertising for positions in over two years. Our whole division is geared to promoting people from within the company and finding slots for displaced workers."

Barbara's is not the only company that has decided it is better to promote people from inside the corporate system rather than going outside for new help. Many companies go through quite an elaborate process of advertising positions on company bulletin boards months before the same jobs are advertised outside the company, if that becomes necessary.

Even if you are comfortable with the position you now have in your company, it's nice to know that you have opportunities to move both vertically and horizontally in your own firm, maintaining your medical and retirement plans while changing your job responsibilities.

Promotion from within serves your company well also. It creates less need for retraining than hiring outsiders and provides beneficial continuity.

To discover whether your company does promote from within, regardless of the formal policy, talk to the people at your level and above. How long have they been in the company? Did they come up through the ranks? If most of the people you talk to were brought into the company as new blood at their current positions, you may want to start looking for a firm that promotes from within.

Quality of Products and Services

It's hard to be happy in a job where you are part of a company that produces shoddy products or gives poor service. It may also hurt your career development if you do not plan to stay with the same company for a good stretch. A receptionist I know, who worked for an engineering firm in Virginia, quit her job because of the daily telephone complaints. Even though she had nothing to do with manufacturing the product that the company sold and had a relatively high paying position, she quit. "I didn't want to be connected with a company that kept getting complaints," she said.

John McGrath, on the other hand, works as a file clerk for Davis and Reuter, an architectural firm. He points out the buildings his firm has designed to all his friends and relatives and clearly is pleased to be with the company.

The value of a craftsman's pride in his or her work is not merely economic. It is spiritual as well, the feeling that you have done the best you could from beginning to end. No matter how well you do your own job in a company, you cannot be proud of your contribution if the end product is of poor quality. Although you may not be able to correct the situation, if you know your company is not putting out a good product or service, you have a responsibility to yourself to find another firm. Staying with a losing outfit does damage to career marketing.

This is not to say, of course, that a stint with a less-than-top-notch company cannot be a valuable learning experience. You may even find that working for such a firm can provide you with worthwhile opportunities to handle many different and important tasks and assignments—since there may not be many other employees who are willing or able to do them well! But, in general, your career will best be served by associating yourself with the most respected companies in your industry.

Corporate Training Programs

You may never have considered corporate training programs as a career marketing tool, but consider this. Each and every time you attend a training session, you are increasing your overall market value. What you learn in those sessions may well support existing or future goals.

I worked for the Burroughs Corporation for only about a year—I had just received my MBA and was frustrated that I wasn't using all the great tools that I had been taught. However, during the course of my year with Burroughs, I was sent to a two-week training school in Lexington, Massachusetts, focusing specifically on sales techniques. That two-week course, in February 1975, has proved more valuable to me than I could have ever imagined at the time. I was a good student and faithfully followed the curriculum the entire time I was there. The methods of prospecting, handling objectives, and closing on sales have become an ingrained part of my overall marketing capabilities and have served me well in every subsequent job and endeavor. In fact, I was able to fuse what I learned into two books.

If you are new to the job market or are considering changing employers, there are two excellent books available on corporate training programs. One is entitled *Breaking In: The Guide to Over 500 Top Corporate Training Programs* by Ray Bard and Fran Moody (William Morrow and Company, New York, 1986). This book provides details on entry level and advance career training programs that launch fast-track careers in a variety of fields. It is written for college and grad students, recent grads, and career changers. Another excellent text is *Inside Management Training: The Career Guide to Training Programs for College Graduates* by Marian Salzman and Deirdre Sullivan (New American Library, New York, 1985). This book profiles 120 companies in more than a dozen career areas and gives contact information on a total of more than 500 corporate management training programs.

In any case, you always stand a chance of approaching your boss with the idea of influencing him or her to send you to training programs you have identified. Those programs should serve the needs of your corporation by increasing your capabilities, and serve your overall career marketing efforts.

Finally, if you learn of a program that you feel you must attend and your organization won't pay for it, pay for it yourself. Over the course of my career, I independently enrolled in Evelyn Wood Speed Reading, the Dale Carnegie Course, an annual convention on community development, an annual writers convention, the Creative Wellness Program, the Forum, an American Booksellers Association Convention, the National Speakers Association Convention, and numerous other events offering seminar workshop and training sessions. Every one of them was worth every penny. There is nothing more incongruous than a potential rising star who is tight with a buck when it comes to investing in his or her career. You have blown a lot of money a lot of different ways, and spending it on training that will offer you a more favorable future is simply money well spent.

Chapter 6

Becoming Indispensable

The only way to find the limits of the possible is by going beyond them to the impossible.

Arthur C. Clarke

Just as an effective marketer creates a niche for the product or service that he or she is promoting, so you must create a niche for yourself in order to advance your career. Creating a niche involves making yourself indispensable, the kind of person supervisors ask for first when reorganizations begin, the office expert on a particular technical subject, or the mentor to many of the company's junior employees. Finding out what's needed on the job (not just what is expected) and doing it will get you noticed quickly.

KEYS TO BECOMING INDISPENSABLE

How do you become the kind of employee your company can't live without? In this chapter, we explore each of the following methods:

Taking the unwanted job.
Going the extra mile.
Working harder when unsupervised.
Getting credit for your group.
Making your boss look good.
Handling key client development.
Becoming a mentor.
Being aware of a supervisor's needs.
Knowing what's needed.

Later in this chapter, we focus on how you can move from being an *indispensable* employee to an eminently *promotable* employee.

Taking the Unwanted Job

Morrie was new to the consulting firm, brought in as one of a well-established group of trainers and instructional designers. Rather than melting into the pot of professionals versed in education, Morrie became an expert in a software spreadsheet program that greatly facilitated project planning.

All of the company's financial records were being changed over to this program. Oddly, most of the firm's professionals had no interest in learning about computers. They viewed computers as the domain of word processing and accounting department personnel.

Morrie, however, saw a niche for himself. The president of the company needed someone who could explain the software program and its applications so that instructions could be given to the accounting department. Morrie stayed after work at least twice a week to become an expert at the software. Soon, anyone with a question about it was referred to Morrie. In short, Morrie became indispensable.

Similarly, you can develop your own niche by picking up a skill or technical knowledge that is vital to your company, yet relatively hard to learn. Be the best at something that no one else wants to do, and you will dramatically raise your level of importance to your organization.

Going the Extra Mile

If you want to get ahead in your company, take on more work than you are assigned. Volunteer to help on a project that is running over deadline and make yourself available for extra projects. You'll be noticed.

Frequently, companies need assistance with rush jobs. At the consulting firms where I've been employed, I always volunteered to work on proposals. Because a quick turnaround is necessary, volunteers are greatly appreciated. Additionally, working on proposals exposed me to information outside of my department and to people I did not work with on a day-to-day basis.

Rachel, a coworker, was called the garbage lady, a name of which she was proud. When a project required short-term assistance to bring it to close, Rachel was asked to take on the extra work in addition to her own project. She was able to switch gears quickly from one project to another and had soon worked with everyone in the company at least once, a unique feat. Her broad experience led to her rapid promotion within the following two years. Although going the extra mile may not always pay off so quickly, the reward will eventually come.

Jane was a new accountant at a mid-size firm. Bob was having family problems and his work had been very poor over the previous few weeks. Jane began to finish Bob's projects, often working until late in the evening. Without bringing attention to herself by complaining or by making it obvious that she was staying late,

Jane greatly helped a fellow worker. This was eventually acknowledged by management as well as her peers.

Going the extra mile can also be done in other ways. Do the little things that make a difference to your project. For instance, I prepared client reports in a company three-ring binder. This was not usual procedure, but I took it upon myself to do this extra work. It made a great difference in the way the reports looked to clients—and to my boss.

Working Harder When Unsupervised

The scene occurs in thousands of offices across the United States every day. The boss is away, on business or vacation. A great sigh of relief goes up the minute he or she is out the door. People drift into each other's offices, the telephones light up with personal phone calls, and lunch hours are stretched to the maximum.

Managers generally report productivity to be only two-thirds of normal when they are not in the office. That is why working, even at your normal pace, when they are away will impress your supervisors.

My strategy during this time, always, was to work extra hard. I knew the boss was likely to monitor employee performance following periods of his absence, rather than while being in the office for an uninterrupted stretch of days.

To add to your indispensability in particular, when supervisors are away, try to complete jobs they assigned before their departure. There is nothing a supervisor appreciates more after a trip than—"Here's the job you wanted. It's done." And the subtle, yet deep-seated message you convey is long-lasting.

Getting Credit for the Group

Getting credit for the entire group of people you work with can advance your career. This seeming irony—standing out by praising the group—makes sense in the overall business context.

Those who make it to the top levels of management are the people who are able to motivate others to do their best and to work well in group situations.

What are you really saying when you say "My team did a great job"? Those above you know that when a group does well, it's at least partly because someone exhibited leadership. Highlighting the team is especially useful when you are managing the group. It indicates your ability to facilitate good work.

Making Your Boss Look Good

Similar to the concept of getting credit for the group of people you work with or manage, making your boss look good can only reflect favorably on you. Both your boss and his or her supervisors will appreciate this.

The best way to make your boss look good is to handle your work efficiently and thoroughly. If your boss is fair, he or she will give you credit for the work, increasing your chances of promotion. If your boss is not doing his or her share of the work, leaning on you unfairly without giving you the credit, it is still likely that you will be promoted when your boss is promoted. That person knows you have been doing more than your share, and he or she will not be able to take a new position without your help. Handling your boss in difficult situations is examined more fully in Chapter 8.

Handling Key Client Development

If your job involves working with clients who do business with your organization, particularly key clients on whom your firm depends, you are already strategically positioned to become indispensable. Each time you interact with the client, either by mail or in person, you are planting the seeds of a personal and professional relationship.

If you've done your job well and have proven time and again

that you are a professional upon whom the client can rely, your relationship with the client, in part, becomes one of your company's important assets. As such, it must be protected just as other tangible assets such as the plant and equipment are protected.

An important caveat to developing key client relationships is not to threaten your supervisors professionally by undermining, overstepping, or otherwise harming the relationships they may have with clients.

Wherever you work, bringing new business into your organization will surely vault you to the head of the class. Whether you have direct marketing responsibility or not, be prepared. Developing new clients is time-consuming and rigorous. However, when you do land a client, surely you'll be the one they trust, the one they've known from the beginning.

Becoming a Mentor

Maybe you're only 28 years old, or maybe you've only been with your present firm for a year and a half. Nevertheless, with your previous experience and achievements, you may already be in a position to serve as a mentor to junior members of your organization. This can be accomplished on an informal, ad hoc basis, and you can literally choose the amount of energy you're willing to commit. Helping junior members always looks good to those above you, especially at performance review time. I always gladly accepted the role of ad hoc mentor to junior associates by distributing reprints of material that I knew was directly helpful in accomplishing their present tasks. At one consulting firm where I was a project manager, I produced a 15-page information resource booklet that I distributed to everyone in the company. This booklet was a compilation of names, phone numbers, and addresses of frequently called libraries, government agencies, and other information services. It was of great use, particularly to junior staff who were not familiar with some of the entities listed.

Now, instantly, they had a complete resource file at their finger-
tips.

Being Aware of a Supervisor's Needs

A primary need of any of us is to be praised. Yet, how often
do we praise our bosses? They are people, too. If your boss has
been extra supportive of you, tell him or her that you appreciate
it. Remember to praise your boss to your coworkers and other
supervisors.

Be honest, however. A phony attempt can be detected immediately. But everyone has some good points that can be
praised.

Be aware of any special quirks your supervisor may have. If
he or she is feeling personally insecure about a particular client
or project, help out and give the credit to your boss instead of
taking it for yourself. You may need similar support some time
later.

Knowing What's Needed

Don't forget the basics. One way to become truly indispensable is to be on top of your job, your department's goals, and
your company's objectives. This three-way strategy includes reviewing your job description, deciding precisely what your department's goals are, and determining your company's objective.
Let's take a brief look at each.

First, knowing your job description and following it, or
amending it if necessary, will protect you from any misunder-
standings. It will also give you an idea of the part you play in the
total picture of the organization, an important factor in your work
satisfaction and chance of promotion.

Your job description should contain *all* the important activities
of your position, the knowledge you must have or acquire to
perform those activities, and some sense of the overall role. (My

book, *Checklist Management: The 8 Hour Manager,* elaborates on what a good job description entails.)

If your job description does not adequately detail the information you must know and the responsibilities you have, now is the time to change it.

Second, be sure to learn and understand the goals of your part of the company. By whatever method your organization is broken into groups—department, division, project team—your group has objectives. As discussed previously, goals are important to guide actions as well as to mark milestones. Knowing your group's goals will help you to set priorities for your own work and to make intelligent decisions concerning how jobs should be done.

Finally, be aware of your company's objective. Any company, from the smallest business to the multibillion-dollar corporation, has an objective. It might be to expand sales, increase mergers, solidify a market already captured, or make a specific contribution to research. If you don't already know, find out your company's objective, or objectives. Your organization's brochure, annual report, promotional literature, or employee handbook should have the objective spelled out. It should unify and give meaning to all the division or department goals. Although conflicts among divisions will occur because of the nature of different responsibilities, a solid base can be produced when all employees realize the overall goal of the organization. Be aware that the objective or objectives can change with differing economic and market conditions. Rapid expansion one year may necessitate carefully controlled stability the next year.

If you are unsure of the direction you should take on a particular project and are not receiving sufficient guidance, look at the problem in light of your company's objective or objectives. Is what you are doing in line with those objectives? Will it be good for the company over the long range? Your ability to make the correct decisions will be greatly enhanced by your awareness of your job description, your group objectives, and the company's goals.

KEYS TO PROMOTION

If you follow the guidelines discussed in the first part of this chapter and become indispensable, are you guaranteed a promotion? Not necessarily. By the same token, making a big mistake in your job probably won't keep you out of the running either. The career track of those who get ahead practically never shows an uninterrupted rising trend line. It's a zigzag—uneven, going all over the place, but eventually hitting the top. However, there *are* some key ways to increase those upward "zags" and parry your job experiences into promotions.

Anticipating Organizational Changes

The usual promotion occurs because someone has resigned or has moved on to another position in the company. In addition to filling such a vacancy, you can create your own promotion by being aware of organizational changes before others are and carving out your own niche in the new structure. As your company expands or shifts its focus, be on the lookout for needs that you can fill on the new organizational chart.

A case in point is Carol, formerly an assistant editor of a hobby magazine. Although she had advanced quickly, her chances for further growth were not good since her supervisor was well entrenched in his position. Recognizing that she needed a chance to grow, she began calling her network of publishing friends and planning the steps needed to get a job with another magazine. Then, from some remarks her publisher made at a farewell luncheon for one of the secretaries, Carol learned that a move was in the works to buy another hobby magazine, about doll collecting. She acted quickly and went to several doll shows in her area, getting ideas from the exhibitors on what they wanted in a magazine. When the publisher sent around a memo announcing a special staff meeting, Carol went to him that day with an organization plan for the new magazine and a table of contents for the first issue. When he reported the acquisition at the staff meeting, he also announced Carol as the new editor. She saw an opportunity and took aggressive, appropriate action to make the best of the chance.

Becoming an Expert

Individuals who become indispensable in carrying out a certain aspect of the company's function will usually be promoted, even if a new title has to be created for the position. Jim became his company's expert on data bases, someone who could answer any question on the topic. His office extension became the hotline for quick information. Because he took over a function that the company hadn't required before, it took some lobbying on his part, but he was named Director of Information. It was a new position in the company and a nice promotion for him.

In your present company, are you developing expertise on a particular topic? If so, make your superiors aware of your special knowledge and the extent to which people depend on *you* to provide that knowledge. Or, if there is an area in which you feel that your department is sorely lacking—perhaps, market research, coordinating functions, or follow-up work—why don't *you* be the one to fill the gap and reap the rewards of career advancement?

Controlling Performance Reviews

In my years as a management consultant, I've come to the conclusion that performance reviews are all too often unfair and useless. Most managers see them as a necessary evil and give their employees only a perfunctory review. However, despite the problems inherent in performance review systems, this is *still* the one time during the year when you and your boss can sit down together specifically to discuss *you*. Throughout my career, I've discovered that it is often possible to turn these matter-of-fact sessions into opportunities for promotion with a little career marketing "homework."

The key is to keep vigilant track of your own performance throughout the year. I evaluate myself quarterly, without fail. All you need do is review your appointment book and your list of goals and other planning aids and compare how you've done versus what you set out to do. Then you can write up your own mini-evaluation using lists and descriptive sentences. Three areas to cover are objectives, skills, and inventory, the latter being simply an overall description of your performance during the last three months.

Armed with your own self-appraisal, you can take more control during the performance review session with your boss. By being able to point quickly to concrete accomplishments, you might avoid simply being labeled with a numerical performance rating, slapped on the back, and sent on your way. More likely, your boss will remember what you've said and will take your case to those higher up in power. An additional perk of the self-appraisal system—no matter what the outcome of your yearly review—is that it keeps you on your toes in your career marketing efforts and may even help you to sell your skills and experience to another company.

Preparing Your Boss

Your boss is vitally important to your career advancement and, as such, must be prepared for such an eventuality. A supervisor who is confident of his or her own abilities and chances for success will be pleased to see you move up. In this case, share your advancement ideas with your supervisor. Let that person know that you want and will work for more responsibility and more independence and that it will look good for both of you to the rest of the company.

Care must be taken, however, with a manager who is afraid that you are after his or her position. People who feel threatened have a tendency to take drastic action to protect themselves. Your forward progress could be delayed by your manager's fear. With such a manager, it is a good idea to try to indicate that your advancement will be a boon rather than a threat. Failing that, you may have to make allies of your supervisor's supervisors and other influential people in the company.

Also consider the needs and desires of your supervisor. Is he or she content with the current position or also looking for advancement? Knowing that will allow you to analyze your chances of taking over his or her job and will give you an idea of the rewards and negative features that such a promotion would entail.

It is well to remember that a promotion does not automatically mean you are advancing along your chosen career path. You can also be promoted to what proves to be a dead-end position or to one that diverges from the path you are seeking.

In evaluating the worth of a promotion, look at two different factors—the overall strength and stability of the company, and the visibility and opportunities of the position to which you are being promoted. Look ahead several positions in the ladder above your current position. If you are an account executive and want to be regional director of marketing, watch the person now in that position very carefully to determine how to respond to situations. "Living ahead" will keep your eyes focused on the correct path and stretch your brain to thinking through the types of situations you yourself will face one day.

Chapter 7

Career Marketing and Office Politics

There's always something about your success that displeases even your best friends.

Mark Twain

Office organization charts always look so nice and neat. Fred reports to Betty who reports to David who reports to Tom ... the lines are straight and direct. That's the *formal* power structure of the company. It's important because it shows who has cemented power and because it is presented to the outside world as the official chain of command.

Charting the *informal* power structure in your office is a much different matter. But knowing it is more important to your career advancement than having a copy of the formal organization chart.

The examples in this chapter will give you an idea of the elements that make up the informal power structure in your office.

CHARTING AND USING THE INFORMAL POWER NETWORK

To ascertain the informal power network, first make a list of the people in your division or department who normally have lunch together. Next to each group, note how long they have been socializing together. Then make notes on how the members of the group can affect your career. Your list might look like this:

Group Members	*Time Together*	*Position/Effect*
1. Mary, Ted, David, Doris	3 months	Project managers; could broaden my horizons, allow exposure to different projects
2. Susan, Judy, Loretta	8 months	Administrative; could help me learn more about company operations

The longer such groups have been together, the harder it will be to make inroads. However, these are the groups likely to have important information.

Next, take note of any small groups that meet behind closed doors but are not working on an office project. It's likely that a shift is in the works. Whether it succeeds or not, keep abreast of its progress.

Pay attention to people who walk into the office of the division or department director without an appointment. No matter where they are listed on the formal organization chart, these people have power.

The informal system is based on relationships among the people in the office. Its foundation is the grapevine—an information system as complete as the telephone company's—because knowledge is power. And power—your ability to make things happen, to control events—is the currency of career advancement. For example, Joan knew by listening to the grapevine that her boss was planning to give an assignment that she wanted to her co-worker, Bob. Joan was disappointed, but she was able to prepare for it rather than hearing the news from her boss and reacting on a gut level to a decision already made. Instead of waiting, Joan approached her boss with a list of reasons why she wanted the assignment, without mentioning Bob at all. She got the assignment.

Listening to the grapevine can let you in on opportunities, crises, and power shifts in advance so that you can plan your responses.

A mentor also can help you understand the power nuances within your company or your field. He or she can teach you skills as well as do you favors. As already discussed, mentors enjoy passing on information, and those years of experience can be very beneficial to you!

Learning from Adversaries

If you're good at your job, you are going to have adversaries. Using that fact to your advantage is a good indication of your ability to play office politics. Understand your adversary's point of view so that your own will become more comprehensive. Is your adversary more conservative about projected costs and time when writing proposals? Does an adversary have different types of relationships with clients?

Analyze an adversary's tactics and use whatever might work for you. How does Judith interact with the boss? What does Todd

say to the secretaries so that his calls go through quickly? Assess
the motives of your adversaries and you'll understand your own
motives better. Do they see the same benefits in the position you
are all seeking?

Author Allan A. Glatthorn, in *Listening Your Way to Management Success*, advises that you listen to your adversary's attacks
on you. Forget any personal feelings engendered by such an attack and listen for the important data that will come out of vituperative remarks—information about how you are perceived
by others.

Lunches, Dinners, and Drinks

Don't isolate yourself by eating lunch at your desk every day.
I did this a bit too often. Lunch conversations can give you valuable insight on peoples' attitudes toward the company, their jobs,
and each other. But it's better to be on the edge of several different cliques than to get tied up with the same group every day
for lunch. Invite someone to lunch from a different division in
the company. Use that time as an opportunity to find out what
that division really does as well as the chance to discover if you
have the same professional interests.

Try lunch particularly if you are having problems with a coworker. The chance to talk over work issues in a different environment, or even to ignore work issues and try a social exchange,
may be all that is needed to smooth the way for the work relationship.

Don't wait to be invited for lunch. Act rather than react. If
someone leaves you by saying, "We must have lunch sometime,"
take advantage of the opening. Call within a few days and suggest
two or three days that you are free. People are more likely to
accept an invitation when it is for a specific date.

Although it's more common for those higher on the power
ladder to initiate lunch suggestions, try inviting an executive

above your level. Surprise moves can sometimes be effective attention getters.

Drinks and dinner after work play different roles depending on your company. At one office where I worked, employees met for beer and chips every other Friday after work. It was good as a morale builder. People whose work didn't bring them in contact through the week would talk and joke during the Friday sessions.

Going out for drinks after work "with the gang" can be a friendly way to show team spirit and solidarity, particularly after a long, involved project. Have a beer, but if the rest of the crowd gets rowdy, stay cool. It's a lot easier to accept an apology from someone who had too much to drink the night before than to have to make excuses for your own behavior.

Being Aware of Body Language

Body language is a rich source of information about relationships in the office. People who lounge in an office door may be demonstrating a lack of confidence about entering the room, or may be indicating to the person inside that they do not have the time to sit down. People standing or walking close to each other are probably allies; people who act friendly but look away while talking to each other or cross their arms are showing their discomfort.

Body language can also be a clue that a person is lying. A study conducted by Dr. Robert Goldstein of New York University and reported in *The Average Book* found that Americans tell an average of 1,000 lies per year. Liars tend to:

Have a brief, minimal change in facial expression.
Cut back on gestures and eye contact.
Lean forward less.
Become self-conscious, shift in their seats, adjust their clothing, and scratch.

Talk slowly and speak in shorter sentences than normal,
thinking that the longer they talk, the more likely they are
to give themselves away. (They are right.)

Certain people—calmer types and men more than women—smile
more when they lie, presumably because this is a gesture they
can control. Other signs, such as a perspiring brow or flushed
cheeks, may indicate that someone is uncomfortable rather than
lying.

Becoming a Company Expert

Become an expert on the formal policies and goals of your
company. Collect all the materials published on company goals,
policies, and statistics.

Roger was new to the public relations agency. Skillful at his
job, he needed a way to fit in with the agency, to create a niche.
A reorganization was underway with a concurrent re-evaluation
of where the agency was heading. By volunteering for a committee to study possible directions, Roger earned the respect of his
coworkers and supervisors while showing that he was capable of
teamwork.

Every organization seems to have certain areas of discussion
or topics that are considered taboo. So, depending on where you
work, it may be necessary to stick with safe talk. What *is* safe
talk? Where my brother works, for instance, all conversations
are banal and focus on sports, weather, or company programs.
Getting into a hot political discussion, however amicable, in the
elevator may sink your advancement plans.

Review any public relations releases about your superiors. If,
for example, civic organizations or country clubs are prominently
mentioned, you know that these activities are valued.

Learn enough about the company rules to know when it's
important for your career advancement to blend in and when to
stand out. Know where the crowd is going and why they are

going that way, without losing your individuality. But most of all, remember that politics is never a substitute for doing a good job.

WORKING WITH THE PRODUCTION STAFF

Other than the self-satisfaction that comes from treating every person with respect, there are several practical reasons for treating your firm's clerical and production staff well. The first is that good treatment tends to get your work done faster and better than the work of a person in the office who does not treat the production staff well. Production staff members may not be unprofessional enough to deliberately hold your work back or do it poorly, since that would damage their own as well as the entire company's reputation, but, nevertheless, take note of the patterns in your own office.

If the typist or person responsible for copying documents feels comfortable enough with you to ask any questions, rather than directing such questions to his or her supervisor who must then relay them to you, the work will obviously get done faster. And, obviously, the supervisor will not be bothered by a lot of questions that you should and can answer.

Another important reason for having the production staff as allies is that they are a valuable source of information. They know who turns in work on time and how complete it is, sometimes more accurately than the person's direct supervisor.

The owner of a mid-size architectural firm says that he learns more by taking the secretaries out to lunch than from weekly progress meetings with his top managers. "They know who is making telephone calls about new jobs, who is slacking off work, who is coming in late, and who makes jokes about me and the other partners," he said.

Members of the production staff also talk to others in the office. One very insecure executive (and there is at least one in every company) played tyrant to the production pool, asserting power that he wanted to have—but didn't—in the organization. Soon everyone in the office was aware of his unnecessary rantings and ravings to the production workers. His reputation quickly declined and he eventually left for another firm.

On the other hand, when a member of the production staff is asked for an opinion on how he or she is treated, good deeds will surely be appreciated and mentioned. The manager of the accounting department wrote a letter to the head of the production department of her company, praising her and the staff for their fast turnaround and accurate work on important financial reports. The accounting manager also mailed a copy of the letter to the president of her company. The president was so pleased that someone had made the effort to notice the work of the production department that he took the accounting manager to lunch. The manager said that, although she had not planned the additional political benefit that came from praising the production staff, she certainly enjoyed it.

Making Production's Job Easier

Accurately estimating the amount of time needed for your job will win you big points with your production staff. If everyone in your office accurately estimates the time needed for production, missed deadlines can be avoided, managers will have more time to review draft documents, and the production staff will have time to do jobs without the mistakes that often happen when something is due "yesterday."

Following are some other pointers to help you win friends on the production staff.

Use the same format.

Large documents are frequently assigned to a number of people, who probably all use different formats. Generate a format at the start of each report and give copies of it to each of the writers. This will make production's job much easier and will require less editing after the first typing.

Make your corrections clear.

Instruct your production staff to return first drafts to you at least double-spaced. Make corrections directly above or below the line in which they are to be placed. Do not turn the page to continue a correction sideways on the page. If a long correction is necessary, add a new page. Ask your production staff what color pens they wish the writers and editors to use. Most typists like red ink.

Respect review time.

Production departments, depending on their size and workload, schedule work carefully. If you estimate three days for review and then take six days before you return the document for a second typing, you are throwing off their schedule. Managers who con sistently do this to the production staff quickly earn a bad reputa tion. Respect the production scheduling process and work with the staff to adjust it only for emergencies. Documents returned for changes more than twice waste production time when the job could have been reviewed more thoroughly the first two times.

Avoid vague due dates.

One kindhearted soul used to frustrate her company's production staff by saying that her work could be typed "anytime in the next three or four weeks." With others in the company having specific due dates, her reports were always moved to the lowest priority. When her due dates got uncomfortably close, the staff would have to work overtime to finish.

Working effectively with your production staff can only make their lives easier, and your life and career advancement smoother.

Chapter 8

When Your Boss Is a Roadblock

Let no feeling of discouragement prey upon you, and in the end you are sure to succeed.

Abraham Lincoln

Hundreds of books are available that offer managers advice on how to handle troubled employees. But many employees find themselves working for managers whose behaviors, procedures, and styles may reduce productivity, create resentment, or demotivate workers. This chapter outlines the ways in which your supervisor may thwart your career advancement, as well as steps you can take to reduce the effects of this unproductive behavior.

RECOGNIZING THE PROBLEM

Do you suspect that you are working for a problem boss? For the sake of your own career advancement, you should be wary of certain types of attitudes and behavior in your immediate supervisor.

Exploitation of Workers

An employee of a software development firm in New England noticed that he was always being assigned to clients located at least three hours of driving time from the office. Although he recognized that on-site work was necessary, other employees in the firm with the same seniority were assigned clients who were within one hour of driving time. For a month the employee kept a detailed log of the hours he spent driving to visit his clients. He also asked two of his friends in the same division to keep similar logs of their visits. At the end of the month, he requested a meeting with his supervisor and pointed out the differences in assignments.

In this case, the supervisor honestly had not realized that he was making assignments in such a manner, and he thanked the employee for bringing it to his attention.

Your supervisor, however, may not be so gracious. If you approach your boss about feeling exploited, be sure that you have a good paper trail documenting your allegations. Phrase your problem in such a way that you allow the supervisor the option of admitting to an oversight. Critique his or her actions, not the supervisor's personality. "It seems I've been assigned a disproportionate share of the overtime work lately, in fact, 20 percent more than any of the other employees in this division. I wondered if you were aware of this?" That approach will undoubtedly work better than if you were to say, "You're sticking me with all the overtime and I'm tired of it."

Manipulative Promises

A frequent trap that supervisors fall into is offering a manipulative promise to employees—the hint or outright declaration that a more favorable future is in store if someone accomplishes a desired goal. Nothing is wrong with making promises dependent on behavior or actions, but some managers may not fulfill the promise once the action has been completed.

If you find yourself on the receiving end of promises that are re-evaluated every time a goal is reached, one way to handle this is to write a memo after a promise has been made. It might say: "My understanding of our discussion this morning is that I will be given a promotion when my sales increase 20 percent over their current rate." This spells out the promise and the action you need to take. Give the memo to your supervisor and keep a copy for use as a gentle reminder if needed.

Closely related to the continuing promise is the dangling carrot. Does your employer ask more of you just before you're due for a raise or a vacation? This form of coercion can, understandably, create resentment. I once had a boss in Connecticut who used to increase my assignments for weeks on end prior to my being due for a raise.

Recognize such behavior, but do not fall into the trap of trying to give more than you've got. A good manager will attempt to maintain an even keel and a balanced workload for you throughout the year. Resist the opportunity to let the supervisor back you into a corner right before annual review time. Continue your work at a reasonable level.

Differential Treatment

If differential treatment is the problem, this is one case where you may not be able to work with your supervisor, but may be forced to go above his or her head. If you are the individual treated unfairly, first attempt to point it out to your boss in a constructive manner. An employee of a small advertising agency felt that she was always given the dirty jobs, assigned to finishing projects that senior associates had fouled up. She openly explained her feelings about it to her boss. He replied that the clean-up work was far from dirty and that he considered her extremely useful to the firm. Her comments, however, made him realize that he had not given her adequate feedback, and he understood her feelings of resentment.

Putting your comments in the light of how the supervisor's behavior makes you feel will often take the heat off the manager, allowing him or her to focus on the behavior itself rather than taking the complaints personally.

If you notice that one or more employees are being treated unfairly, you should point this out to your supervisor. You might bring this up by saying, "I notice that Sam and Ellen seem to feel that you treat them differently from the rest of us. I know you don't mean to do this, but I just wondered if you noticed?"

Although there's a fine line between intrusive and helpful behavior, closing your eyes to unfair treatment of fellow employees can backfire on you. You may one day fall out of your supervisor's favor and end up on the receiving end of the same type of treatment. It will be better for you, and your organization, if all employees are treated consistently.

Programming for Failure

This practice is particularly damaging, not only to employees, but also to the overall company productivity and reputation. Supervisors "program for failure" when they give assignments that cannot be completed successfully or when they do not provide sufficient guidance or resources to finish the task.

The first step in avoiding programming for failure is to know your own work schedule. How much can you accomplish in a given amount of time? What resources do you need to complete a certain job?

If you are given an assignment with a built-in time bomb, point this out immediately. Don't wait until a day before the project is to be completed before letting your supervisor know that it was impossible from the start. Once you realize a project in progress is in trouble, write down all the facts and make as close an estimate as possible of the resources and time necessary to save the project.

An associate of mine who was frequently caught in this trap designed her own weekly progress report. This allowed her to chart the time and resources used for each task, letting her supervisor know the problems in advance as well as providing a good baseline for estimating future projects.

Inconsistency and Inflexibility

Does your supervisor sometimes alter the meaning of something that was said previously? Poor supervisors can get in the habit of "bending" what was assigned or said to suit their own current needs. It is obviously impractical to carry a tape recorder at work to catch every word your supervisor says. But you can ask for further explanation of assignments or statements. Try asking for a repeat of the assignment a day or two after it has been given. Your supervisor may have altered the assignment in his or her mind without telling you.

The flip side of the inconsistent manager is the one who is overly rigid when issuing assignments or maintaining work schedules. In the changing workplace today, many employees have needs for flexibility in both the hours that they work and the order in which assignments are due.

If you have a valid reason for wanting to change a supervisor's order, first think through the benefits to you and the company (or client) before asking for such a change. Showing that increased productivity will result will usually get your supervisor's admiration for your logical thoughts, rather than resentment that you are trying to change orders without a reason.

Little or No Feedback

Unfortunately, it often seems that some supervisors have trouble giving feedback on positive developments, and no trouble offering feedback on problems. A lawyer friend once told me that his firm had not given him a raise in two years because of financial problems. He was unhappy about the lack of a raise, but he was more unhappy about not getting any feedback about his performance. "I would've gladly stayed with the firm if they had given me regular performance reviews and explained how I was contributing to the firm. I could live without the extra money if I knew how I fit into the company's future."

Feedback, both positive and negative, is vital to your performance and fosters an atmosphere of trust and cooperation. Most supervisors who don't give feedback are not intentionally creating trouble. Some people just are not in the habit of commenting on performance.

In that case, ask for it! As you hand your supervisor a report, say, "I'd like to hear your thoughts on this." If none are forthcoming in a reasonable time, ask again. It may take some time to "retrain" your employer to give you feedback.

A very frustrating trait of some managers is to answer questions for feedback with one word, such as *fine.* Point out with tact that you value your supervisor's experience and would appreciate specific positive or negative comments that could improve your performance.

Another way to condition your supervisor to give more feedback, and also to practice your office politics, is to give the supervisor appropriate feedback. How many of us compliment our bosses on work well done? It's easy to forget that managers need feedback, too.

TURNING THE PROBLEM TO ADVANTAGE

Your boss might be a terrible taskmaster, a tyrant of the office, insensitive to individual needs, or just plain callous. He or she may be routinely morose, unsupporting, or guilty of exploiting workers. The list of management sins could go on and on. However, most of the people who complain daily about their bosses don't realize that there are actually some benefits to working for a boss that they don't respect. And there are ways to turn a bleak situation to your advantage.

Following are a number of things you can do to change the problem of having a poor boss into a boost for your career.

Strengthen Your People Skills

Working for a boss whom you do not respect will most assuredly strengthen your ability to deal with people—including good and bad future bosses—and it will hone your diplomacy skills as well. If you can learn to peacefully coexist with people whom you do not respect, your chances of successfully dealing with all others will improve. This is an important side benefit for career marketers.

In a study of top level executives conducted by Korn-Ferry (with the University of Southern California), it was determined that one of the single most important traits for making it to the top was the *ability to get along with others.*

Take a More Active Role

When your supervisor is an incompetent boss who lacks creativity and has difficulty making decisions, you can turn the situation to your advantage by taking on more of an active role. Do some of your supervisor's work by thinking up solutions to problems and new programs or products. Be careful, however. If you do this, be sure to share your ideas with your boss first instead of taking them to colleagues or to your boss's boss!

Get Some Perspective

Perhaps you're working for an insensitive boss who, intentionally or otherwise, calls you on the carpet for minor mistakes or takes credit for your achievements while neglecting to praise your efforts. It may seem that nothing positive can come from this experience, but don't despair. You are learning one of the most valuable of business lessons—"don't take it personally." Nothing stops a career dead in its tracks more than the tendency to take every callous remark or each lack of recognition as a personal affront. Successful career marketers don't dwell on these things; they move on.

Keep Cool

Having a pressure cooker for a boss can be a nightmare and is certainly the cause of many an ulcer. However, rest assured that you are not the only one who notices your manager's volatile behavior. The strategy, then, in the face of his or her explosions, is to strive to be a model of calm level-headedness. Your ability to stay cool and perform well, contrasted with your boss's temper tantrums, should eventually win you kudos from colleagues and from top management.

The "Plus" of a Negative Example

It may sound like a cliché, but you can learn as much from a negative example as from a positive one. A friend of mine in the publishing business is constantly praised by his subordinates for his management style. When asked to what he credits these glowing reports, he told me that he kept meticulous mental notes of what his previous boss had done wrong, and he vowed to do the opposite when he was in a position of authority. So, instead of wasting mental energy grousing about the things your boss is doing wrong, it might pay you to think about how they could be done right in the future.

If You Must Move On . . .

Sometimes, of course, a bad boss can make your life so unpleasant and unrewarding that you simply have to escape the situation. Once you have determined that you can no longer stay in your present position (beyond the short run), you may find some comfort just in knowing that you are leaving. If, for any reason, you have ever debated for months about leaving a position and you now find yourself confronted with a boss for whom you know you cannot work, you'll probably regard this situation as beneficial.

All your mental anguish can subside, because as soon as the right position develops, you are going, and you know it. There is light at the end of the tunnel. The daily drudgery and personal contact that you have eagerly sought to minimize are now, at least, palatable. The strains and pressures that may have followed you home can now diminish.

Once you have made the decision to go, however, make sure that your energies are focused on procuring the next position. Don't dwell on why you are going or how good it will be when you are gone. Also, although the chances are at least fair that you will gain a new boss whom you can respect, remember that there is also a chance that things could be worse.

Forget Sweet Revenge

As long as you remain in your present position, continue to do a good job and uphold the name of your organization. To do anything else would be a strong reason not to respect yourself. Be professional and take your experiences in stride. Learn and benefit from them, but do not waste your energies resurrecting the past. Don't try to "even up" the score or fulfill your personal sense of justice. It would be a waste of time, regardless of any minor psychic satisfaction. The long-term personal benefit to career marketing in gaining "revenge" is nil. Moreover, the possibility of something going wrong or being misinterpreted is high. When you must leave, do it with dignity and class. That attitude will pay off in the long run.

Part III

Interpersonal Skills to Support Career Marketing

_____

Chapter 9

Good
Marketers—
Good
Listeners

A fresh mind keeps the body fresh. Take in the ideas of the day, drain off those of yesterday.

Edward Bulwer-Lytton

We learn how to read, speak, and write as children and are encouraged to expand these skills throughout our lives. However, we seldom, if ever, receive any formal training in listening or pay attention to its importance in our lives.

According to researchers at the University of Minnesota, people spend 45 percent, or nearly half, of their communication time listening. Good listening is an active, complex process that takes knowledge of a few basic tenets and lots of practice. In a professional or personal relationship, it pays to sharpen your listening skills.

The first time I truly became aware of my listening shortcomings was during a meeting with one of my mentors, Dick Connor, in 1981. Connor had the habit of taping meetings and key conversations. We would meet every couple of months to discuss a new article and identify the key points. Every time we sat down at Dick's dining room table, he would have the tape recorder and a spare tape ready. He would turn it on and then get to work. Later I took the tape home and reviewed it. I was amazed at the number of gems and insights that came up during the discussion that I had simply forgotten about. Had that tape not existed, clearly over half of what we had discussed no longer would have been available to me. Even my prodigious notetaking did not come close to capturing what that simple cassette tape could capture.

In time, I stopped taking notes during the meeting and instead just focused on the interpersonal communication. I discovered that the best time to take notes was later, while slowly reviewing the tape. Soon I developed Dick's habit without his ever suggesting I do so. I began taping key conversations, client interviews, and speeches. The technology is perfect—when the information is no longer of value, simply tape over. If the information is of great or lasting value, make a copy.

The lesson I learned from taping conversations was that no matter how well I thought I listened, I was still obviously missing a lot and it was likely that those around me were missing a lot also.

What Is Active Listening?

"Active, as opposed to passive, listening involves not merely taking in the words of the speaker but trying to grasp the facts and feeling behind them," according to an article titled "Identifying and Overcoming Listening Problems" by William G. Callarman and William W. McCartney, published in *Supervisory Management.* Active listeners respond in a conversation by stating their impression of what the other person is saying. Psychotherapists have long used this technique because it reassures the patient that the therapist has understood, and it encourages the person to open up.

Let's say that Joe is the president of a small research and development firm. He believes that his sales manager, Kurt, is taking on too great a share of the work, decreasing overall efficiency among the sales team. Joe is practiced in active listening. He invites Kurt into his office, asks his secretary to hold all phone calls, and offers Kurt a cup of tea. (Attention to those details is important in setting up an atmosphere where a useful conversation can take place.) Following is a conversation between Joe and Kurt that illustrates the major points of active listening.

> Joe: Kurt, it seems as though your sales team members have been able to take it pretty easy lately while you seem overworked. Have you noticed that?
>
> Kurt: Actually, I guess I have been working a little harder than usual. I have to do everything myself though. I can't trust those guys to do things right.
>
> Joe: So, you're saying that you're the only person who can handle accounts with the proper amount of care?
>
> Kurt: Yes. Harry was late on delivery of two reports for our biggest client. The reports were done. Harry just didn't deliver them on time.
>
> Joe: You're a little jumpy about the rest of the team then because of Harry's mistake.
>
> Kurt: That's right. They acted like it was no big deal.

It's easy to see that Joe is going to get to the bottom of the problem using active listening techniques. Joe never makes suggestions for solutions. He merely repeats what he thinks Kurt said, and what he meant as well. Paraphrasing does not imply agreement of what is being said, just acceptance that the other person has a right to that feeling or statement.

Active listening is good for business for a number of reasons. Supervisors who are active listeners show that they believe their employees have experience, ideas, problems, and solutions that are worth attention. This helps subordinates gain respect for themselves and for their supervisors.

Spontaneous contributions from employees tend to increase as each person feels comfortable exposing his or her ideas before the supervisor and the work group. Cohesiveness produced by this increased comfort level can be good for profits. Research has shown that the relationship between cohesion and productivity is very strong.

Active listening also keeps others off the defensive, gets problems out into the open, calms down angry people, prevents mistakes made by those hearing only part of a customer's order or a supervisor's request, and establishes strong relationships.

Barriers to Effective Listening

Dr. Chester L. Karrass, director of the Santa Monica, California-based Center for Effective Negotiating, offers several reasons why we don't listen as well as we should.

- We often have a lot on our minds, and it's not easy to switch gears quickly to fully absorb and participate in what is being said to us.
- We have adopted the habit of talking and interrupting too much and not letting the other party continue even when it may be to our benefit.
- We are anxious to rebut what the other person has said, and if we do not do so readily, we are afraid we may forget our point.
- We allow ourselves to be easily distracted because of the setting or environment in which the meeting takes place.

- We jump to conclusions before all the evidence has been presented or is available.
- We discount some statements because we don't place importance on the person presenting them.
- We tend to discard information that doesn't match what we want to hear or that we don't like.

Dr. Karrass points out that "poor listeners often drop out of a conversation with the hope that they will catch up later. This seldom happens." If you find your mind wandering away while listening, make a conscious (and repeated, if need be) effort to focus on the conversation.

Another very important reason that we don't listen as well as we should is that the average person speaks at a rate of 125 words per minute. The average listener can process between 400 and 500 words per minute. Because we are able to think so much faster than the normal speaking rate, it is easy to let our minds race ahead of the speaker, not focus on what is being said, or appear disinterested. The faster our ability to process information, the greater the potential to practice daydreaming or other bad listening habits. Good listeners use the lag time to make mental summaries of information presented and notes of ideas to pursue later without losing focus on the conversation.

HOW TO EVALUATE LISTENING HABITS

The following checklist, developed by Richard C. Cupka, former director of the Institute for Leadership Education at Purdue University, will help you to evaluate your own listening habits.

Do you give the other party a chance to talk?
Do you interrupt while someone is making a point?
Do you look at the speaker while he or she is talking?
Do you impart the feeling that your time is being wasted?

Are you constantly fidgeting with a pencil or paper?

Do you smile at the person talking to you?

Do you ever get the speaker off the subject?

Are you open to new suggestions or do you stifle them immediately?

Do you anticipate what the other person will say next?

Do you put the other person on the defensive when you are asked a question?

Do you ask questions that indicate that you have not been listening?

Do you try to out-stare the speaker?

Do you overdo your show of attention by nodding too much or saying yes to everything?

Do you insert humorous remarks when the other person is being serious?

Do you frequently sneak looks at your watch or the clock while listening?

This is a tough checklist, and anyone who is willing to reflect honestly will undoubtedly discover several areas for improvement. Consider also the ten keys to effective listening in Figure 9–1.

At Sperry Corporation (now Unisys), generally regarded as a corporate leader in the development of listening skills, former CEO and chairman, Gerald G. Probst noted that listening is more than just "a corporate slogan." Probst called it "a philosophy of business," relating it to both managerial efficiency and the bottom line.

"Business is finally taking seriously the costs of poor listening, those little mistakes that waste time, cause embarrassment, irritate customers, alienate employees, and, ultimately, affect profits," said Probst. "Until recently, few people realized the major role that listening plays in managerial efficiency. Fortunately, that's changing. Many firms, such as Sperry, have added listening

Figure 9–1. Ten keys to effective listening.

Ten Keys to Effective Listening	The Bad Listener	The Good Listener
1. Find areas of interest.	Tunes out dry subjects.	Opportunitizes; asks "What's in it for me?"
2. Judge content, not delivery.	Tunes out if delivery is poor.	Judges content, skips over delivery errors.
3. Hold your fire.	Tends to enter into argument.	Doesn't judge until comprehension is complete.
4. Listen for ideas.	Listens for facts.	Listens for central themes.
5. Be flexible.	Takes intensive notes using only one system.	Takes few notes; uses four or five different systems, depending on speaker.
6. Work at listening.	Shows no energy output; fakes attention.	Works hard; exhibits active body state.
7. Resist distractions.	Is easily distracted.	Fights or avoids distractions; tolerates bad habits; knows how to concentrate.
8. Exercise your mind.	Resists difficult expository material; seeks light, recreational material.	Uses heavier material as exercise for the mind.
9. Keep your mind open.	Reacts to emotional words.	Interprets color words; does not get hung up on them.
10. Capitalize on fact that thought is faster than speech.	Tends to daydream with slow speakers.	Challenges; anticipates; mentally summarizes; weighs the evidence; listens between the lines to tone of voice.

training to their employee-orientation and management-development programs."

Even if you are a great listener—and there are only a few—you won't reap the full benefits of listening effectively unless you let your audience know how well you have listened. How can you do this? After someone has spoken to you, ask pointed questions, reflect on something that they have said, or discuss action that you will take as a result of their message. Following are some good tips from Arnold "Nick" Carter, of the Nightingale-Conant Corporation, on what you can do to actively improve your listening capability:

- Listen for key words that give you the clue to the main thrust of what is being said.
- Control your emotions throughout the listening experience.
- Analyze what has been said, what is really meant, and the thrust of the communication.
- Be sure you are tracking logically and accurately as you listen.
- Outline as you listen to see how the pieces fit.
- Have fun listening and feeling yourself growing and understanding during the process.

Remember that good listening skills take time and practice. Follow the ten keys to good listening in Figure 9–1, ask yourself the questions regarding your listening habits discussed earlier, and open your mind to what other people are saying. It could be the most important skill you have developed in years.

Chapter 10

Honing Your Communication Skills

Life is an adventure in forgiveness.

Norman Cousins

Communication is an exchange—a simple but vital concept. Yet, all too often we approach interchanges with no consideration of how the other party will react. Our own message looms large, overshadowing the person with whom we are communicating.

Cultivating an awareness of how the other person is likely to react to your communication is key. Next, create identification with the other person. In addition to putting that person at ease, it will open your mind to his or her perceptions and reactions—a vital part of communication.

Donald J. Moine, of Redondo Beach, California, a psychologist who heads his own sales and management training firm, compared the sales techniques of high-achieving and mediocre salespeople. Moine found that *top sales personnel instinctively match, with hypnotic effect, the customer's voice tone, rhythm, volume, and speech rate.* Career marketers should take note.

"The good salesman or saleswoman matches the customer's posture, body language, and mood," explains Moine. "If the customer is slightly depressed, the salesperson shares that feeling and acknowledges that he or she has been feeling a little down lately. In essence, the top sales producer becomes a sophisticated biofeedback mechanism, sharing and reflecting the customer's reality—even to the point of breathing with the customer."

The technique works because "hypnotic pacing" helps establish trust and rapport. It does not work as a gesture, however. Anything other than an honest attempt to understand the other person and his or her frame of reference in a particular situation will be seen as mimicking, which will lessen trust.

Whether writing a letter, speaking with a coworker, or telephoning a client, consider that person's likely mood and reaction. What effect is your message likely to have? And how can you phrase that message for maximum benefit?

COMMUNICATION LEVELS TWO AND THREE

According to Lyman Steil, a speaker and author on communication, we all communicate with each other on four levels. The first level is small talk, informal conversation. The second level is catharsis—venting feelings and sharing problems and frustrations. The third level is the exchange of information, the level most of us use during the typical business day—talking over strategies or passing on facts. Persuasion is the fourth level. People generally warm up to this level, beginning with small talk and going on to level two or three, finally trying to convince you to change your mind or sell you on an idea.

In the first part of this chapter, we are primarily concerned with honing your skills at levels two and three. Later, we focus on level four because proficiency in persuading others will be the most helpful level to you in your career marketing efforts.

Improving Communication Skills

First, remember that you can only learn by listening. Listen carefully, rather than thinking of your next statement or question. *Let* yourself be interested rather than *trying* to be interesting. When it's your turn to speak, such open-ended questions as "What could be done to strengthen this report?" will encourage responses. Saying "I need help" or "I don't know" often shows strength, not weakness.

Tape a few meetings in your office. The tapes will not only point out your listening shortcomings but will also help you to analyze your own communication patterns. Listen for such details as your rate of speech, stridency, and tonality. Your voice should be pleasant and varied enough to remain interesting.

Are your transitions logical or do you jump from one subject to the next? Do you monopolize the conversation? The most important question to ask yourself as you listen to the tapes is: "Was the conversation a useful exchange of ideas?" If not, try correcting some of the communication patterns you heard that were destructive to the exchange.

Establishing eye contact is vital to opening up a line of dialogue with another person. Think back to uncomfortable situations you have been in during your career. Were you looking down or away from the person speaking? Was the other person constantly focusing at a point somewhere over your shoulder?

Staring at someone, of course, is usually taken as a threat or an insult, but a direct, clear gaze is important.

Notice people who are trying to get your attention, such as political workers at the entrances to polls or volunteers for charitable funds during Christmas or other holidays. Before they say anything, they try to establish eye contact. Looking down, hunching your shoulders, and hurrying away will usually dissuade them from attempting a conversation. But once they have caught your eye, it's almost a sure thing that you will listen to what they say.

Salvation Army "Santas" claim that they almost always get a donation if they make eye contact with pedestrians. Salespeople who use eye contact with customers generate more and larger sales. The same goes for working in the business world. Managers and executives who use their eyes when talking with their staffs open up communications and are able to get more work done.

An important tip to remember if you are leading a meeting is to get there in time either to talk to or establish eye contact with, and nod to, all the people attending. They will feel more like participating and you will have the opportunity to gauge their moods.

Making the Most of the Telephone

You wouldn't think of walking into someone's office and starting a conversation without first knocking. Yet, people do much the same thing every day on the telephone. Always give the person the option to call you back later if the present seems not to be a good time.

Since you can't see the other person, which generally counts for a great deal of our information during a conversation, ask extra questions about how the person feels about what you are saying. When you call an office and the person is not in, leave a complete message. You should give your name, title, organization, and a brief sentence about why you are calling.

Joe Stumpf, co-owner of Automated Sales Training, has produced a video tape that offers 29 techniques for professional use of the telephone. Titled "It's for You ... Your Most Important Call," here are some of the tips it offers:

1. Answer the phone on the second or third ring, if possible. Your goal when answering the phone is to make the caller feel important and comfortable, and you have about 15 seconds to make a lasting first impression.
2. Never start your phone presentation with an apology. You lose all control and positioning.
3. Answer your phone with enthusiasm. Enthusiasm is positive—it's contagious. Place a mirror next to your phone. Before you answer, look in the mirror and say, "I answer my phone with enthusiasm."
4. Smile when you talk. You sound happier.
5. Develop a sincere and positive attitude. People know when you're faking it.
6. Speak slowly. The normal rate of speech is 150 words per minute on the phone. Slow down to 100 words per minute.
7. Have empathy. Listen. Let them know you understand.
8. Don't interrupt.
9. Take notes. This will help you remember important points.
10. Listen for the overtones.
11. Use the caller's name. It is, for him or her, the sweetest sound in language.
12. Be proud of yourself and your position. How you feel about yourself is heard in your voice.
13. Pause!
14. Show you're grateful and appreciative. Say "thank you."

Reading Nonverbal Clues to Conversation

One advantage you have when speaking in person rather than on the phone is that you can read a person's nonverbal clues. Any time that interpersonal communication takes place, there are nonverbal clues in the conversation. The effective career marketer should become aware of and constantly monitor various body language signals, such as personal distance, posture, and gestures.

Personal distance.

How far away does the other party stand? A normal space zone between two people in a business transaction is 4–12 feet. But everyone's space zone may differ. Monitor any changes during a conversation or over the course of many conversations that may indicate a change in the attitude of the person.

Posture.

Is the other person standing tall (exhibiting confidence) or slouching (possible defeat, depression, or lack of confidence)? Notice your own posture when speaking to different people in your office. Do you stand differently when talking to your supervisor versus a coworker?

Gestures.

Are the person's gestures consistent with the spoken message? If your supervisor praises your work while turning away from you to look out the window, the messages are inconsistent. You would be safe to take the nonverbal gesture—looking away— as the more accurate one, since we are in more conscious control of our verbal, rather than nonverbal, statements.

Whether you like to or even want to, especially when you're

at work, you are communicating all day long. By becoming more aware of this dynamic process and the verbal and nonverbal clues that you send to bosses, coworkers, and the office staff, you can better position yourself to relay the type of message you choose.

LEVEL FOUR—SELLING YOUR IDEAS

The great nineteenth-century author Robert Louis Stevenson said that "Everyone lives by selling something." But could that really apply to *everyone?* Surely not to a newborn baby, for instance, or to a nun. Or could it? A newborn baby sells love, affection, and hope for the future to parents, relatives, and siblings. A nun sells the love of God, love of humanity, and the spirit of brotherhood and sisterhood for all. If you are married, you have already made the ultimate sale—convincing your spouse that it would be in his or her best interests to share a life with you.

What about selling at the workplace? Charles Porter, a partner with the Big Eight accounting firm of Coopers and Lybrand, often refers to a bit of wisdom he was once privileged to hear, which essentially says that between any two people, at any given time, one is selling something to the other. This is a serious statement and one that can easily be misunderstood.

Think about it for a moment. Whether you are with your boss, a coworker, production staff, a member of your family, or a friend, hundreds if not thousands of "sales" are occurring all the time. Shall we meet at 9 o'clock or at 10? Should the report include the extra exhibit? Should we choose this restaurant or that? In order to resolve such questions, one person undoubtedly influences or obtains agreement from the other. So, even if the actual position you presently hold does not remotely involve formal or designated responsibility for selling, you will nevertheless advance in your career by improving your salesmanship.

Charging with Enthusiasm

Dale Carnegie probably said it best about half a century ago when he remarked that "Enthusiasm is contagious." The enthusiasm you possess for your current task, projects on which you work, your job, your organization, your community *is* contagious. When you become excited and enthusiastic about what you are doing, you will more readily gain the interest and participation of others. Approach the same task with a lackluster "who-gives-a-darn" attitude and absolutely no one will want to help you.

Have you ever noticed that some of the most successful people that you know are motivated by powerful slogans and phrases? My late father, who was the vice principal of a junior high school, used to win people over the second they entered his office. His walls were filled with pictures of great Americans such as Abraham Lincoln and Martin Luther King, and slogans and phrases that he would sometimes refer to and draw upon when working with a troubled adolescent.

This does not mean that you should necessarily decorate your office with "rah, rah" slogans and uplifting plaques, but a glance through Bartlett's familiar quotations and other similar books can greatly help in your career marketing efforts. Slogans and phrases can empower and help to energize us. I keep several such books by my desk, and whenever I find enthusiasm or energy waning, or I need to get charged up to make a "sale," I spend a minute or two with these powerful passages. Here are three of my favorites:

> All men dream but not equally. They who dream by night in the dusty recesses of their minds wake in the day to find that it is vanity; but the dreamers of the day are the dangerous men, for they act their dream with open eyes, to make it possible.
> —*T.E. Lawrence*

> In this culture you have to define yourself very strongly and
> clearly or people won't see you . . . I have dreamed my own
> self into being. If we collectively dream a future, together, we
> can obtain it.
>
> —*Alice Walker*

> Enlightened men living in a democracy readily discover that
> nothing can confine them, hold them, or force them to be con-
> tent with their present lot.
>
> —*Alexis de Tocqeville*

Try reading such a phrase or slogan, any that may particularly
appeal to you, just before you have to make a presentation, or
when you have made an unpopular decision that you know to be
right, or just because you want to. Even the most enthusiastic
among us often suffer some "down time." Powerful statements
tend to recharge our batteries.

Sales Start in Your Mind

No matter what your position in your present organization,
to whom you have to report, and whom you must influence to
get ahead, selling, as we have discussed, is an essential component for your career success. All top earners in professional selling agree that the sale, any sale, starts in the seller's *mind*. When
you are firmly convinced regarding what path to take, what strategy to follow, then you are ready to effectively convince others.

Abraham Lincoln was once asked by a young student what it
would take to become a lawyer. "Young man," said Lincoln, "if you
are firmly convinced that you are going to become a lawyer, then
you are already halfway there." And so it is with your sales effort.

One potential entrepreneur from southern California experienced eight years of continued failure, as one bank after another
continued to reject his loan application for an innovative recrea-

tional project that he had conceived. At one point, this "dreamer" had to declare bankruptcy, but in the end his selling effort prevailed. His name was Walt Disney.

Hazards of Overselling

The biggest! The greatest! The newest! The fastest! The best!

As a consumer you probably stay away from products that make too many claims like those. And they don't work so well in the office either. David H. Sandler, a sales seminar trainer from Stevenson, Maryland, believes that, contrary to popular conceptions, the most influential and effective salespeople sell softly. The marks of a "super" salesperson, according to Sandler, include:

- Bringing up objections before the other party thinks of them.
- Concentrating on what will sell the idea while not trying to overimpress.
- Spending the first part of the meeting finding out about the other party's problems.
- Spending much of the meeting time getting the other party to suggest how the problem might be solved.
- Making a presentation tailored to the other party's needs.

Remember that whether you have ever considered yourself a salesman or saleswoman or not, consider now that you indeed are. Over the years, selling has taken on a rather negative connotation. Yet, it is selling that turns a depressed economy around, and it is selling that enables your organization to continue to exist.

Chapter 11 _____

Boosting Your Self-Confidence

While doubt stands still, confidence can erect a skyscraper.

George Lorimer

Self-confident people radiate power and health. Others want to be around them and to be like them. Self-confidence, however, is a skill you can practice. The concept gets little notice sometimes because people who don't have self-confidence confuse it with egotism. On the contrary, it is most attractive because self-confident people make other people feel that way also.

Self-confidence is the man who walks into a job interview knowing that he has the skills and knowledge to handle the position being offered. Self-confidence is the woman who asks to be promoted based on an assurance that the promotion is deserved because of past work. Self-confidence comes from feeling that you deserve to have and be what you want.

Why Is Self-Confidence So Important?

Self-confidence is a prerequisite to success and happiness since performance is based so often on attitude rather than aptitude. Success or failure can become a self-fulfilling prophecy. This is particularly true in the area of self-marketing. For example, if you want a promotion or a raise but are not really confident that you deserve it, you are likely to let your doubts get in your way. You may be reluctant to directly approach those in charge of promotions. Or, you might couch your request in a vague, indirect manner, using such terms as "maybe," "if," and "sometime."

A confident person applying for a new job writes a cover letter that states "I will do x, y, and z for your company," and "I look forward to hearing from you." Such statements imply right from the start that the applicant will be interviewed and will be hired. The less confident applicant couches the correspondence in terms of "I could do x, y, and z for your company" and "I hope to hear from you." These statements, on the other hand, imply doubt. In the mind of whoever reads the letter, that doubt easily extends to the applicant's appropriateness for the job. Confidence means taking a positive approach—an approach that has a way of rubbing off on other people.

Confidence also can help increase your effectiveness through the idea of positive reinforcement. If you expect to do well at any particular endeavor—from performing a task on the job to achieving social acceptance outside the job—you are likely to do far better than you would if you expect mediocrity or failure. Teachers have known for years that students who are told they are progressing well in spelling, math, or whatever tend to achieve far more than students who are told they are having problems. Doubts compromise your effectiveness, and self-doubts make it unlikely that you can effectively market yourself. It's like trying to sell a product you don't believe in. You can't commit yourself to it wholeheartedly.

How to Become More Attractive

Self-confidence increases your attractiveness to other people, and that, in turn, also can increase your effectiveness. So much of what we do—at work and outside work—is done with or through other people. When they sense that you are confident, they want to be around you, support you, and even be like you. They "go to bat" for you and generally assist you in being as effective as you can be. It makes them feel good to be around someone who has a positive, enthusiastic, "can do" attitude. On the other hand, people tend to shirk away from someone who is continually worried, self-doubting, and skeptical.

Peace of mind and contentment with life are possible only through acceptance of yourself, which will lead to acceptance of others. Many forms of destructive behavior can be traced to lack of self-confidence. For instance, a midlevel manager at a high technology firm constantly befriended new employees, only to spread rumors about them later. This man, unsure about his own place in the company, felt it necessary to destroy the reputation of new employees. Obviously, such behavior could only destroy his own position in the long run.

Confidence seems to create a resiliency that allows you to bounce back from failures. Positive self-esteem provides a reservoir of inner strength—a constant that is not dependent upon others and the situations in which you find yourself. Conversely, lack of self-esteem saps your energy with worries about acceptance and accomplishments, creating a downward spiral when those worries really do begin to hamper your effectiveness.

Building Self-Confidence

First, you are *not* stuck with your present degree of confidence. If you have ever found yourself thinking "I'm just not a very confident person," you are wrong. Confidence is not handed out at birth; it can be developed. Of course, developing it is hard work, even lonely work. When you begin to work on becoming more self-confident, you may not get a lot of support from others. Do it anyway; they'll come around sooner than you think.

A major step in building self-confidence is to take a good look at the roots of your lack of it. Where does it come from? In what situations is it more problematic? In what situations do things seem a little better? Finding the answers to such questions can help you dispel personal myths, emphasize positive occurrences, and begin a realistic program to build your confidence.

In my case, I spent years convinced that I wasn't as smart as a lot of other people. Even though my record in high school was way above average, I felt that I could never compete with my truly brilliant friends. Until I was about 30 years old, I was certain that really brilliant people, like some of those I had known in high school, were not at all uncommon, and, of course, I would never quite achieve that lofty status. I finally realized that my brightest school friends were not actually representative of the entire population as a whole. Simply understanding the roots of my lack of confidence—and dispelling some myths about it—bolstered my own confidence enormously.

I find that it helps to determine the exact situations in which one feels more or less confident. Don't just worry about them, write them down; and continue by writing a plan of action for improving the situation. For example, your action plan might look like this:

I feel most confident when. . . .
I feel least confident when. . . .
Some things I can do to improve a situation of least confidence are. . . .

Here's how one person completed the above:

I feel most confident when I know I am wearing clothes appropriate to the situation, when I am physically fit, and when I am

Figure 11–1. Confidence questionnaire.

1. I tend to complete tasks successfully that I wholeheartedly attack. _____
2. I feel uncomfortable about the amount of formal education I've had. _____

3. I check and recheck to make sure I have done things even though I really know they were done. _____
4. I have frequently wished that I could act more spontaneously more of the time. _____
5. I have no qualms about meeting new people of either sex. _____
6. Sometimes it seems that everyone is seeking my opinion on something. ___

7. The one word that best describes me in my childhood and to some extent today is *inadequate.* _____
8. I have always regretted that I could not live up to my parents' expectations for me. _____
9. I get enough feedback at work to know that I am performing satisfactorily.

10. I have often found myself thinking self-condemning thoughts. _____
11. I feel that I don't have the right to criticize anyone for anything because I have my own failings. _____
12. I feel a sense of accomplishment from my work. _____
13. Basically, I accept and respect myself for the person I am. _____
14. I often find myself worrying about what others are thinking about me. ___

among people I know well. I feel least confident when I am among strangers and when I feel I have taken on more than I can achieve in a given time frame. To improve a situation that instills low confidence, I need to look and feel my best, to be highly organized in my work, and to operate under the assumption that everybody suffers a certain amount of discomfort in a room full of strangers.

You can also gain a lot of information about your personal level of confidence by examining how you act and react at home, at work, alone, and in the company of others. In Figure 11–1, the questionnaire used by lecturer Sam Reed Horn is designed to help you pinpoint situations that may have precipitated feelings of low self-confidence. Indicate true or false after each statement. (Add a little explanation if you like.)

. It isn't difficult to review your answers and see where some problems might lie. For example, if you answered false to #9 (I get enough feedback at work. . . .), you may sense a lack of confidence at work that stems from ambiguity about your performance. In this case, the remedy may be in taking the initiative to ask for feedback. This is particularly likely to boost your confidence, because the people performing badly generally get plenty of feedback. Another example: If you answered true to #2 (I feel uncomfortable about the amount of formal education. . . .), your lack of confidence in this area may mean that you expect to achieve less than your educated colleagues, and, therefore, *do* achieve less. Many great achievers throughout history had very little education.

Practice Confidence-Building

Beyond analyzing the sources and situations concerning your level of confidence, there are some specific strategies you can adopt and steps you can take to learn and practice confidence-building:

Set reasonable expectations.

Practicing self-confidence will not change you into wonder-woman or superman overnight—or even at all. Self-confidence will only allow you to make the best of what you *can* do.

Know what you do well.

Your confidence may be so low that it seems you do nothing really well. But stop and think about even the small things that you do each day—from organizing your mail to meeting self-imposed deadlines for routine chores. You may be surprised to find some abilities and positive features that you haven't given ample credit in the past. Making a list works well. You'll find that by emphasizing the positive, you'll gain confidence to work on the less positive.

Please yourself.

Extending yourself just to impress others runs counter to the idea of confidence. You may need to spend more time doing things simply because *you* want to do them and they make you feel good. These are the activities in which you are most likely to succeed and that are most likely to bolster your confidence when they go well.

Look for small victories.

Maybe you didn't get that promotion, but pat yourself on the back for getting asked your opinion in a meeting or for completing that report ahead of schedule. Don't figure "all is lost" if the big accomplishments elude you for now. If everything seems to be falling apart in one area of your life, look for achievements in another.

Reward yourself.

Enjoy your successes. Celebrating success helps you take the focus off your mistakes. When you finish a budget or report on deadline, take yourself—and others—out to a movie. When you get some long overdue positive feedback, treat yourself to a lunch hour at a museum or buy yourself a book you've been wanting. Let other people know you are celebrating and that they are important enough to you that you want them to share.

Learn from mistakes.

Don't let mistakes drag you down by dwelling on them. Instead, regard them as lessons—steppingstones that give you a higher vantage point for better knowledge and wisdom. Be glad that you've learned that lesson and will not make that mistake again. But, give yourself permission to make some mistakes and to be a little less than perfect.

Sound confident.

Practice using positive terms in conversation. For example, no matter what internal doubts you may have, simply say, "Yes, we will get that done" or "I can get it finished on time." Your confidence will likely lead to a better chance of accomplishing what you've said you will do. Practice speaking without saying "but," "maybe," "if," "I'm not sure," and other uncertain words and phrases.

Look confident.

No matter how you feel today, dress and groom yourself as you would on a day when you were feeling on top of the world. Remind yourself to stand as if you want to be an inch taller and walk with a firm, purposeful stride. When you keep your head up and maintain good eye contact, those around you act more interested and confident in you. And that, in turn, will build *your* confidence.

Initiate conversations.

It's not easy simply to start talking to people you don't know, but force yourself to do it. We all start as strangers. What's the worst that can happen? They are unlikely to turn and run away or to act insulted or angry. Starting a conversation with a stranger at a conference or a party will build your confidence, because they will generally respond with interest and gratitude. People will view you and treat you as a self-confident person.

Prepare discussions.

Play through any upcoming scheduled meetings, interviews, or conversations ahead of time. This prepares you to handle most obstacles that could arise. Write some notes to yourself about topics, questions, and responses. If you're at a loss for words in social situations, make some mental notes about all the topics of "small talk" for which you could ask questions or initiate discussions. These might range from the weather to the front page news. What you say may not be as important as the fact that you are able to say something with confidence.

Imitate self-confident people.

Identify the people around you who seem to have a good degree of self-confidence and watch what they do. I find this technique to be particularly effective. Is it how they work, what they say, how they carry themselves? Select just one small behavior at a time and try to emulate that. Dr. Judy Kuriasky, former radio talk show host, says, imitation is essential to learning. She notes that if you are attracted to self-confidence in others, it's likely that you have the capacity for greater personal self-confidence. The qualities we admire and envy in others usually reflect our own undeveloped capacities.

Experiment with roles.

In the privacy of your home, preferably in front of a mirror, act out the self-confident attitudes and manners that a really confident person would show the world. A friend of mine once related that he has eight different hats, ranging from a baseball cap to a Texas ten-gallon hat. Every morning, he puts on a different hat depending on what challenges he will face that day. Then he pictures his meeting those challenges while he looks at himself in the mirror. Use whatever works for you.

Increasing your self-confidence primarily is a matter of finding out what makes you feel good about yourself and then practicing the relevant behavior patterns. It means assuring yourself and others that you have made and will continue to make some very worthwhile accomplishments—without shrugging off any accomplishments as "too insignificant to count." As you display this attitude more and more, others will soon increase their confidence in you. And that will lead to even greater self-confidence on your part.

Part **IV**

Special Tools to Forge Ahead

Chapter 12

Reading and Career Marketing

Every society needs a continuous flow of new ideas.
Henry Steele Commager

Although you may not have considered it before, reading is a vital component of your career marketing effort. Most of what you know about your career and your industry is obtained from reading. Indeed, in order to become an authority in your field, there are certain basic types of information that you must have, and mastering your reading will make this ongoing task all the easier.

Successful executives read and seek out industry data to help them support their views both within and without their organizations. They manage their professional reading as if their careers depended on it—because they do. However, as business professionals, we face a daily avalanche of reading materials, subscriptions, and junk mail, and it is difficult or impossible to maintain a reading schedule for work-related requirements. Is keeping pace truly impossible, or is there a way out of this reading morass?

Keeping Pace

If you could talk to supervisors and business professionals throughout the country, you would soon realize that professional reading is regarded as an important component of the job and career, yet there is seemingly no time, or precious little, that can be allotted for it. In addition, the number of quality business, career, and management publications has more than doubled since the mid-1970s, only adding to the confusion over what to read and when to read it.

Start Somewhere

The first step you can take is to redefine, or perhaps more accurately define, the type of information to which you *need* to be exposed, and what type of information can be readily discarded or ignored. I started to realize that unless I figured out what I must read, what I might read, and what I like to read, I would remain hopelessly deluged. Key publications and sources of information that supply you directly with what you need to know are to be preferred over passive sources—those publications such as the daily paper, general interest periodicals, and much direct mail material that take up more time than they're worth.

If the notion of giving up the daily paper or dropping some of your favorite subscriptions leaves you cold, take heart. Everyone needs some pleasure reading. The question is how much and when. If you're skeptical as to how much time can be saved or allocated for active reading, test yourself over the next 30 days. Briefly skim the paper or read only the Sunday edition or a weekly newsmagazine. Listen to more radio and TV reports while you are doing something else, such as driving or eating. Once you give up cover-to-cover reading of the daily paper, you will probably wonder why you ever developed that habit in the first place.

Skimming and Scanning

If you did not master "skimming and scanning" in high school or college, it's not too late to learn. Skimming involves perusing the first one or two sentences of a paragraph within an article to see if the information in the paragraph is pertinent to your immediate quest. Skimming can also be used when you are confronted with several journals or periodicals at the same time. The basic payoff to skimming is that it enables you to quickly determine whether or not you should invest more time in the article or the publication.

Scanning is a technique used with large volume materials. Often I have to research several books or periodicals for the purpose of extracting key information. Scanning enables me to effectively handle the task in a short time. Scanning involves reviewing the table of contents, index, list of charts and exhibits, and occasional paragraph leads to determine what, if any material is of interest. The availability of high-speed photocopiers greatly facilitates the scanning process since you can capture directly what you need.

Of course, both of these techniques can be enhanced by speed reading. By moving a pencil under the text as quickly as your eyes can follow, yet still reading the words, you can almost double your skimming and scanning rates.

Reading at a Desk

Virtually every kind of professional-type reading is more effectively undertaken sitting at a desk rather than a chair, couch, or even a table. At a desk you have ready access to stationery, envelopes, scissors, pens, pencils, ruler, and all other office supplies that enable you to clip, tear, send for, save, and file what you've read. I also find it very useful to start a "clip" file of articles that interest me and to review this file periodically to see what ideas take shape.

Many professionals, surprisingly, feel guilty about reading at the office desk. The guilt seems to stem from the fact that reading at the desk does not appear to be productive; it certainly doesn't cause one to perspire. Many people erroneously believe that if they are not in some form of motion, they're not really working. If this is a problem for you, you may wish to discuss the need to read at the desk with your boss and with your coworkers or staff.

Your professional reading is an important part of your job and you *deserve* the right to read at your desk. However, even if there is no stigma attached to the act, you may still find it difficult in the midst of the office hustle and bustle. If you haven't done so before, now may be a good time to allocate a number of hours per week for uninterrupted professional reading at the office. Many professionals choose to do this very early in the morning or late in the day. The time is not important. What is important is that you don't kid yourself into thinking that you can read, absorb, and apply important data or information while surrounded by noise.

Delegating Reading

You may not have considered it previously, but a stack of periodicals you've been wanting to get through or those key chapters in the latest book or those reports that have been piling up don't have to be read by *you* at all. If you have any employees who report to you, some of your reading can be delegated to your staff, including the most junior. All that is necessary to effectively delegate some of your reading workload is to provide clear instructions as to what you're looking for and how you want it presented.

Perhaps you only need to have a few key paragraphs under-lined. Maybe you need a one-page listing of pros and cons on a certain issue or procedure. Properly convey your objectives in the delegation of reading material.

MAKING READING MORE PRODUCTIVE

One method of reducing the time invested in reading while increasing your real return is to drop all of your subscriptions to those publications that can be found in your local library and that largely contain articles and information that need not be read immediately. Thus, every few months you can skim several issues of selected periodicals, copying or retaining only what's actually needed. Don't hesitate to delegate the copying, too. I found that after I dropped several subscriptions, I didn't miss the publications at all! And when I wanted to see what topics they had been covering, I could review several issues at a time in the library.

Data Bases

Subscribe to one or more of the various bibliographic data base services that quickly and conveniently afford you the ability to skim the contents of hundreds of current and dated periodicals across the broad spectrum of industries and professional disci-plines. *Management Contents,* for example, provides a hard copy or terminal display of the contents tables of hundreds of business and professional publications every two weeks, for a relatively nominal fee. Their address is:

Management Contents
FIND/SVP
500 Fifth Avenue
New York, NY 10036
(800) 323-5354

   Other on-line data bases, such as Dialog, ABI, and BRS, provide an impressive array of information arranged by periodicals,
subject, author, and numerous other cross-references. These services also provide instant bibliographies for selected topics and yield
informative, well-written article abstracts, or, if so desired, entire
article reprints (the fee for reprints is high, usually $7–$12).
   Dialog, CompuServe, and virtually every other data base and
data base service can be located by using one or more of the
following directories:

Computer-Readable Databases
American Library Association
50 East Huron Street
Chicago, IL 60611
(312) 944-6780

Directory of Online Databases
Cuadra Associates, Inc.
2001 Wilshire Blvd. #30
Santa Monica, CA 90403
(213) 829-9972

Federal Database Finder
Information USA, Inc.
12400 Beall Mountain Road
Potomac, MD 20854
(301) 983-8220

Data Base Directory
Knowledge Industry Publications
701 Westchester Avenue
White Plains, NY 10604
(914) 328-9157

Data Bases for Business
Chilton Book Company
Radnor, PA 19089
(215) 964-4000

The North American Online Directory 1987
R.R. Bowker Co.
245 West 17th Street
New York, NY 10011
(212) 645-9700

Also, the *Source Directory* is an annual listing of over 5,000 sources of business information. It includes many publishers of data bases.

Source Directory
Predicasts, Inc.
11001 Cedar Avenue
Cleveland, OH 44106
(216) 795-3000

Jeffrey Lant, in his self-published book *Tricks of the Trade* (JLA Publications, Cambridge, MA), reviews several data bases of interest to those wishing to master their business reading and information-gathering capabilities.

Book Review Services

Your reading time can be reduced greatly by employing one or more of several excellent book review services. Sound View Executive Book Summaries, for example, capsulates leading management and business books into four- to eight-page summaries and offers new titles every month. Contact:

> Sound View Executive Book Summaries
> 100 Heights Road
> Darien, CT 06820

Another service is the *Wall Street Review of Books.* This periodical is available four times per year for a very reasonable fee. For more information write to:

> *Wall Street Review of Books*
> Redgrave Publishing Company
> 380 Adams Street
> Bedford Hills, NY 10507
> (914) 241-7100

Check the current edition of *Literary Marketplace*, R. R. Bowker & Co., New York, NY for a complete listing of book review publications.

Newsletters

Newsletters have become a valuable source of information. They are now published by government agencies, industry groups, associations, political groups, and virtually every corporation. The *Oxbridge Directory Newsletters* lists several thousand newsletters, arranged by functional area. The *National Trade and Professional Association Directory of the United States* (NTPA) indicates which of the thousands of associations listed maintain a newsletter. The *Newsletter Yearbook* is also a valuable guide. By accessing these directories and others that your local librarian may suggest, you can gain access to late-breaking news and information of concern to your business and industry.

There are also many management, communications, and business newsletters that effectively scan what you may have chosen to scan yourself. Two are listed below.

Topline
13–30 Corporation
505 Market St.
Knoxville, TN 37902
(615) 637-7621

Communication Briefings
806 Westminster Blvd.
Blackwood, NJ 08012
(609) 227-7371

Newsletter Directories

If you're interested in reviewing a wide range of industry newsletters, the following directories can be helpful:

Standard Periodical Directory
Oxbridge Communications, Inc.
183 Madison Avenue, Room 1108
New York, NY 10016
(212) 689-8524

(Lists over 72,000 magazines, journals, newsletters, directories, house organs, association publications throughout the United States and Canada.)

Oxbridge Directory of Newsletters
Oxbridge Communications, Inc.
183 Madison Avenue, Room 1108
New York, NY 10016
(212) 689-8524

(Lists some 5,500 newsletters in the United States and Canada.)

National Directory of Newsletters and Reporting Services
Gale Research Company
Book Tower
Detroit, MI 48226
(313) 961-2242

(Lists thousands of newsletters issued by commercial and non-commercial publishers.)

Newsletter Yearbook/Directory
Newsletter Clearinghouse
44 West Market Street
Rhinebeck, NY 12572
(914) 876-2081

(Lists 2,600 newsletters offered through subscription.)

If you have a computer and modem, you can subscribe to hundreds of other business-oriented newsletters, even if you are not a subscriber to any of them, through NewsNet. This is an information delivery and retrieval service that produces electronic editions. Current newsletter issues, and back issues for the past year, are stored in NewsNet's main computer. By dialing a local telephone number, NewsNet users access that data base. They pay a modest rate to read the newsletter. A small minority of newsletter publishers also impose a surcharge for those who are not subscribers to the printed version of their newsletter.

There are two other NewsNet features available without additional charge. Subscribers are able to scan headlines only, allowing them to be selective with the articles, thus reducing time charges. Additionally, any newsletter, a combination of newsletters, a date, a combination of dates, or the entire data base can be searched by key word. You select a word or words and order the computer to search for articles containing that word or words. It then tells you which articles contain the word or words selected, allowing you to scan headlines or read the articles. More information is available from:

NewsNet
945 Haverford Road
Bryn Mawr, PA 19010
(800) 345-1301

Listening to Learn

Your reading time can be further reduced by using your ears. Subscription cassette services such as SuccessTrax, Newstrack Executive Tape Service, and Listen USA greatly accelerate your information gathering capability. SuccessTrax, for example, features interviews and information from 10–12 leading authors, speakers, and executives from around the world—all presented in an enjoyable format. The Newstrack Executive Tape Service abstracts and summarizes, on tape, key articles from leading business and management publications. Listen USA offers over 60 different programs of approximately 45 minutes in length, including book adaptations, seminars, and small group discussions on the leading business, professional, motivational, and self-help topics of the day from the people that have actually "been there." For further information, contact:

SuccessTrax
P.O. Box 1357
Winchester, VA 22601
(703) 877-1191

Newstrack Executive Tape Service
Box 1178
Englewood, CO 80150
(800) 525-8389

Listen USA
60 Arch Street
Greenwich, CT 06830
(203) 661-0101

Many other tape cassette services are available. Consult the business reference librarian at your local library or at a local university.

In summary, the old slogan that your grammar school teacher posted on the wall has been true all along—Readers *are* Leaders. And those who find ways to absorb more vital information in less time will have more time to lead.

Chapter 13

Writing and Career Marketing

The more I want to get something done, the less I call it work.

Richard Bach

If reading is the first special skill to support your career marketing efforts, then the second is writing. There are standard written materials or tools that you should prepare to support your overall marketing efforts. These include a biography, news releases, articles, and fact sheets. As you will see, each can be a vital tool in making yourself well-known in your business and in the community at large.

The Up-to-Date Bio

A biography is not a résumé. A résumé is certainly useful for landing a new job or in the preparation of proposals, but it is somewhat inappropriate in career marketing. A biography differs from a résumé in that the biography is written in the third person as if someone were talking about you; it is not necessarily organized by chronology or function; and it should be composed in an upbeat, lively, and yet authoritative manner. The biography in Figure 13–1 is my own (as of January 1987) and is shown as an example.

When and where do you use a biography? Biographies should accompany any articles that you write, may accompany any press releases about you, and certainly should be included with any other information that you send when in contact with members of the media. As a general rule, any time that someone requests information about you, other than when you are in a job search, your biography, rather than your résumé should be sent. To submit a résumé when a biography is called for is a strong indication to the receiving party that you are not adept at career marketing.

My bio is constructed primarily to accent the books I have written and secondarily to focus on my speaking and consulting services. If any part of my bio is truncated when published, my books are still likely to get mentioned. Later on, when we discuss getting on radio and TV (Chapter 21), you will find that your bio can also be used by media hosts whereas a résumé cannot.

News Releases

In 1981 I discovered the press release. Up until that time, I didn't realize that pictures and little blurbs that appeared in the paper each night about local dentists, lawyers, and business executives were submitted by them. I actually believed that there was a roving reporter seeking out tidbits from the business and professional community.

Figure 13–1. The biography.

About the Author

Jeffrey P. Davidson, CMC, of Falls Church, Virginia, is author of five books—*Checklist Management* (National Press, Washington, DC), *Marketing Your Consulting and Professional Services* (John Wiley & Sons, NY), *Marketing to the Fortune 500* (Dow Jones-Irwin, Homewood, IL), *Getting New Clients* (John Wiley & Sons, NY), and *Blow Your Own Horn* (AMACOM Books, NY).

He is a featured speaker at conventions and seminars on marketing professional services. As a CMC—Certified Management Consultant awarded by the Institute of Management Consultants—he has obtained the management consulting industry's high accreditation.

Jeff's award-winning articles appear in both U.S. and international publications, including *Marketing News, Journal of Professional Services Management, Computer Decisions, Business and Society Review, Washington Business Journal, Washington Post, Inc. Magazine, World Executive Digest, Rotarian, Management Quarterly, Training, Toastmaster, Today's Office, Working Woman, Business Horizons,* and others. This year his articles will reach more than 12 million business professionals.

His achievements gained him area recognition as the U.S. Small Business Administration's "Media Advocate of the Year" in 1983, 1984, 1985, and 1986.

He has made hundreds of presentations from Maine to Hawaii. He is represented by Capital Speakers Inc. of Washington, D.C., who also represents Louis Rukeyser, Ellen Goodman, Jim Palmer, and James Reston. He has appeared on CBS Nightwatch, radio, and cable television (Warner AMEX).

Jeff has a BS in marketing and an MBA from the University of Connecticut. He is a designated Connecticut State Scholar, and is listed in *Who's Who in Finance and Industry* and *Outstanding Young Men of America.* He was cited as an American Institute of Management "Executive of Distinction," an award also given to Rep. Jack Kemp; Irving Shapiro, former Chairman of the Board, E.I. DuPont De Nemours & Company; and Alonzo G. Decker, Jr., Chairman, Black & Decker Manufacturing Company.

☐ Photo enclosed. Please return to:

> Jeffrey P. Davidson
> 3709 S. George Mason Drive, 315 E
> Falls Church, VA 22041

The average person simply does not realize that the media needs him or her. Newspapers are constantly looking for stories and press releases that they can run to fill their pages. Looking in the papers and seeing what others had sent in made me realize that every other thing I was doing could also be worked into a news release.

Much has been written on how to prepare a news release. Essentially, a good news release contains information organized according to the five W's: who, what, where, when, and why, plus how. It is written in the "inverted pyramid" fashion; the most important information is presented first and the small details at the bottom. The release must be easy to read and snappy; don't make any sentences too long or it will lose the editor right from the start. Models of successful news releases—those that have been published—are far more instructive than explanations. See Chapter 18, Becoming Your Own Press Agent, for samples of news releases that were accepted and published.

Writing Articles

Writing articles for publication is a highly proactive strategy for marketing your career (discussed in greater detail in Chapter 17, Breaking into Print). If you have ever considered writing an article but hesitated, be assured that it is not nearly as difficult as you think. Most publications routinely edit your material. They are far more interested in receiving interesting themes and interesting concepts submitted by people with the right qualifications.

Regardless of your field, you undoubtedly have information that will be of interest to your peers or the clients your industry serves. Don't make the mistake that so many others make by thinking "who would want to read something written by me?" This is a defeatist and unrealistic attitude. With thousands of magazines, newspapers, journals, and newsletters in print, more than one million "bylined" articles appear in the United States alone each year. A significant number of those are by first-time authors. As our society becomes more technologically sophisticated, the potential to get an article published will increase dramatically.

Facts on Fact Sheets

Fact sheets have been used successfully by businesses who wish to highlight a particular product or service in a simple, cost-effective way. They can also be used on the personal level in support of your overall career marketing efforts. A fact sheet is no more than a one-page list of data about yourself, a topic on which you are an expert, or the product or service you offer. Fact sheets can also be in question-and-answer format. Fact sheets are particularly useful for a high-gear self-marketing strategy such as getting on radio and TV. The fact sheet represents an important element of a media or press kit. An example of a good fact sheet is shown in Figure 13–2.

Organizing Your Materials

Organization is essential to enable you to manage all of the paperwork involved. If you don't already own one, it will probably make good sense to buy at least a two-drawer (preferably a four-drawer) filing cabinet. Effective career marketers recognize that organization of marketing materials is essential. If you own a personal computer and have a good letter-quality printer, perhaps you can do without the filing cabinet. Either way, there is no escaping the reality that effective career marketing requires substantial organizing.

My own filing cabinet, for example, has a section on outlines of speeches that I give frequently. Another section contains all of the hard copies of article manuscripts and still other sections on proposals, correspondence, and letters of commendation.

I am probably more cautious than most because I keep a disk copy and hard copy of all of my materials. Any of the popular

Figure 13–2. The fact sheet.

SALES
DYNAMICS
INSTITUTE®

224 Carnation Court
Baltimore, Maryland 21208
(301) 484-8933

JACK COHEN. . .

SOME BACKGROUND

INFORMATION

JACK COHEN

PRESIDENT OF SALES DYNAMICS INSTITUTE

Jack Cohen is currently an instructor in the marketing department at the University of Baltimore, where he teaches personal selling. As the director of Sales Dynamics Institute, he conducts its regularly scheduled sales skills training workshops, specializing in the SDI Selling System and the selling techniques and management strategies necessary to use this new, innovative, and relevant selling style.

Since 1951, he has been a specialist in marketing, selling-skills training, sales communications, management consulting, and marketing-support systems. He is an author, professional speaker, and seminar leader who has lectured for the academic and business communities in colleges, conventions, banquets, and workshops for multi-level audiences.

For 14 years, he served as a corporate officer and the director of marketing for a prominent, publicly owned company with divisions in five mid-Atlantic states employing 80 salespersons who produce more than $50M.

word processing programs available are adequate to store your career marketing materials.

Dictating Equipment

As a supervisor, project manager, and author, I've discovered that when it comes to writing longhand, dictating to a secretary, or even using my own word processor, the difference between those methods and using portable dictation equipment is akin to walking up stairs versus taking the elevator in a tall building. Once one becomes familiar with the ease of dictation operation, the convenience, and the pure joy of finishing reports in approximately one-third the previous time, there is no returning to the old methods. For instance, those who compose directly on a typewriter or word processor may type 40–80 words a minute. The writer struggling with longhand can usually write only 20 words per minute. With a little practice, a person can dictate 100–140 words a minute—six times as fast as words can be captured in any other fashion, regardless of how fast you can type.

Whether you type or write, the problem is that while you are thinking, your mind races ahead of your fingers. Many of the ideas and phrases you compose in your mind can be lost. The arithmetic is simple; the logic undeniable. Portable dictation equipment enables you to tackle all the things that you have wanted to write, but never found the time in which to do so.

Are you still unconvinced? Then try the following test. Time how long it takes you to write these sentences in longhand:

All else being equal, a portable dictation equipment user has greater career potential than those who don't indulge. Starting tomorrow, why not try some models?

Could you finish in under one minute? If you did finish in under a minute, is it legible? The above sentences contain only 25 words. Pausing numerous times while dictating, you would still complete them in about 25 seconds. Proficient users could finish in under 15 seconds.

Dictation can be used for almost *all* of your writing needs, from lengthy reports and letters to memos and notes to yourself. Just about anything that takes more than five minutes to write should be dictated.

A common misconception.

Despite the obvious efficiency of dictating, many business executives and supervisors don't use dictation equipment and offer this rationale: "I like to see what I'm writing in progress." A visual review is helpful, but it is *not* necessary. If you think that you can't write without being able to visually review what you've written, remember that a good outline is a prerequisite to effective writing—whether writing longhand or using any other method. When dictating with a good outline, key words can readily be expanded to sentences and paragraphs. The pause feature on all portable dictation equipment allows you easily to start and stop to gather thoughts and to articulate complete sentences and paragraphs. Moreover, several brands of portable dictation equipment offer recall and playback features that allow you to monitor the recording as it progresses. With a good outline, however, the need to review what has been dictated diminishes in direct proportion to use of the equipment. It takes only two to four hours to become proficient.

The need for visual review is generally overestimated. As one writes longhand or relies on the word processing screen, the desire for visual review increases due to the relatively slow progression. The human brain works faster, much faster. In other words, writing longhand or monitoring a screen reinforces one's feeling of great need for visual review. But dictating in 20- to 30-second blocks what may have previously required two to five minutes to write negates the need for visual review.

Mike fright.

Jefferson D. Bates, author of *Dictating Effectively: A Time Saving Manual,* points out that another big obstacle business people need to overcome before using dictation equipment regularly is "dictaphobia." To overcome dictaphobia, he says, "you must recognize that putting words on tape is just as easy as talking to a spouse, neighbor, or office associate." He recommends the following steps in overcoming the fear of speaking into a dictaphone:

- Pick a subject you know well.
- Jot down a few ideas on the subject in outline form.
- Study the words for a few moments, while the ideas sink in.
- Pick up the cassette recorder, close your eyes, and take several deep breaths. (This helps put you in a creative state of mind.)
- Imagine you're talking to a close friend or associate, anyone you feel comfortable with and trust. Picture that person in your mind.
- Start talking. If you still have hang-ups about getting started, take something you have written earlier and start reading it aloud onto the tape.

As these thoughts may have suggested, there's yet another advantage to using dictating equipment. Once you become accustomed to the process, it can encourage unmatched creativity in your writing. The speed and freedom it offers can make it much easier to capture fleeting ideas—and that's sure to pay off in concrete benefits to your career.

Chapter 14

Your Internal Achievements List

It's lucky for people who aim high that most people have no aim at all.

Walter B. Pitkin

You may not view yourself as a high achiever, but your achievements are probably more substantial than you think. Most of us are so accustomed to what we do and what is expected of us on a day-to-day basis that we don't think of many of our activities as real "achievements." We're surprised when someone else is impressed with something we've done that seems rather ordinary to us.

If you are really interested in achieving more, you need to start by recognizing the achievements you have made—and then build from there. The achievements you have already made will help encourage you to strive for future ones, so you need to stay continually aware of them. Shrugging them off with modesty or forgetting about them will just make it harder for you to add more achievements to your repertoire.

Perhaps you're thinking that achievement isn't really such an important deal anyway. On the other hand, if you decided to read this book, you probably have a fairly high need and desire for achievement.

The Achievement Motive

David C. McClelland, after years of research in the field of motivation, identified three major factors that motivate people to varying degrees: the achievement motive, the affiliation motive, and the power motive. Most people have one of these as their dominant motive, although some individuals are high in all three.

In studying the achievement motive in particular, McClelland determined these characteristics about people who are primarily motivated by achievement:

- They want to accomplish something significant.
- They like to set their own goals.
- They are eager to be their own boss, as they do not like having people tell them what to do.
- They gravitate toward sales, marketing management, and independent businesses.
- They tend to be loners.
- They do not readily seek advice or help, but are willing to listen to experts only.
- They tend not to have high sensitivity toward others.
- They are not high in human relations abilities.
- They are self-motivated.
- They want full responsibility for attaining their goals.
- They are always figuring the angles, taking calculated risks.

- They prefer to select moderate goals for themselves—*practical* challenges, as they want to win.
- They want immediate feedback on how well they are progressing toward their goals—such as sales, bonuses, concrete measures.
- They are not motivated to work harder by monetary incentives, but they do want to be paid well.
- They come mainly from middle-class families that set attainable goals and are supportive of their children.

The achievement-motivated individual, then, is quite different from the affiliation-motivated person, who is inspired by close interactions with others and good personal relationships. Likewise, the achievement-motivated individual differs from those who are motivated by power—striving for the status and authority that come with getting to the top.

McClelland believes, and has successfully shown in his own training programs, that people can be taught the achievement motive. As they acquire strength in this area (although the other two areas of motivation probably will not be completely absent), they tend to become more self-confident, more enthusiastic about what they might be able to accomplish through their work, and more able to take carefully calculated risks.

In other words, being motivated to achieve is good—especially to stimulate challenges and enthusiasm at work. People with very low or completely absent achievement motivation may find their work and their lives empty of vitality and vigor.

Keeping a List

One of the best ways I have found to keep myself in perspective about my achievements and what I want to achieve is to keep an Internal Achievements List. I developed this list as a way of helping me to be a "consultant" to myself—to readily see gaps and problems, as well as successes.

I keep the list in chronological order, divided by month, over the span of a year. At the end of a year, I can see what I have (and haven't) achieved. Most of us would be surprised at just how much we do achieve in one year, and writing it down is generally the only way to keep track. I restrict my list to those activities, awards, milestones, and the like that really signify to me that I've accomplished something. However, whatever is an achievement for you—whether or not that achievement is recognized by others—should be included in your list. For instance, you might regard finishing a project three days ahead of deadline as much an achievement as getting an award for the same project.

Here is an example—part of my Internal Achievements List for 1984, my last year as a full-time employee before becoming my own boss.

January: Appeared as one of 18 presentors at the National Capital Speakers Association's first annual Speakers Showcase for area association, corporate, and government meeting planners and executives. Elected to the Board of Directors of National Capital Speakers Association and assumed responsibility of secretary through May 1984.

February: Made an appearance on Warner Amex Cable TV Station Channel 8 in Reston, Virginia, as guest on Association Focus, hosted by James Fleckenstien, which focused on how job seekers can use professional and trade associations to greatly enhance the job search process.

March: Selected as the 1984 Media Advocate of the Year for the District of Columbia by the U.S. Small Business Administration.

April: Cited by the American Institute of Management as an Executive of Distinction in the field of management.

May: Interviewed for feature article by the *Christian Science Monitor* on streamlining your life through goal setting and personal time management.

As you can see, my Internal Achievements List reads like notes to myself, and that's exactly what it is. I don't attach it to résumés or send it out with biographical materials when I make speeches or write articles. However, even though use of the list is strictly internal, it has wide-ranging spin-off benefits. For example, after I made up the first such list, I soon began developing news releases around my monthly achievements, something I probably couldn't have done "off the top of my head," without the encouragement of first seeing some achievements written out all in one place. Those news releases, in turn, helped my visibility.

The Internal Achievements List gets you moving and keeps you on target. Some of the major benefits of keeping, and frequently reviewing, such a list are noted below.

Gauging progress.

Seeing your achievements all in one place, in chronological order, helps you determine whether you are making the kind of professional and personal progress you have in mind for yourself. You can readily see the kinds of things you have achieved that are supportive of your goals, versus achievements that might simply take up time and energy without moving you toward those goals.

Getting the attention of others.

If you already have a very clear picture of your accomplishments, you are way ahead in terms of letting your boss know why you should have that raise or promotion. It also helps an interviewer to know why you should have the job. You can promote yourself well when you know yourself well.

Supporting external documents.

Your internal list can be very helpful when it comes time for you to draft a résumé, a biography, or other materials about yourself. The entire process of putting your abilities and history in writing is streamlined when you already have written out some of the most important factors.

Projected Achievements Log

Once you have mastered the process of putting your achievements in writing, it makes sense that projecting achievements into the future could also support your progress. The achievements that go into this log are the ones you really think you can accomplish, again chronologically by month. Many of these can be drawn from your list of career goals.

In determining your likely achievements a year into the future, you need to be realistic. Don't just list everything you *think* you'd like to accomplish; stick to those items that you feel you have a *reasonable* chance to accomplish. On the other hand, don't "hedge your bets" by developing a very short list that only includes the safe items and none of the achievements you would really have to strive to complete. This list should also act as an incentive to spur you on, keep you on track, and remind you when you've taken a detour. If it is too optimistic, it will be discouraging and you will shelve it. If it is not optimistic enough, the possibilities won't stimulate you.

Following is an example of a Projected Internal Achievements list:

January: Will complete and submit an article for publication. Will devise new secretary support system.

February: Will serve on at least one panel for the XYZ Society annual meeting. Will submit my name for one ongoing task force.

March: Will gather information for an article while on business trip to Portugal.

April: Will take out a summer membership in the local racquet and golf club and begin to network with business associates there.

May: Will complete application for national professional certification. Will speak to a student group touring Denver.

June: Will develop plan to split my department in two, with me as head of one of the new departments. Will gather documentation to support this change from inside and outside the company.

July: Will submit proposal to my boss and other top officials. Aim to receive my best-yet annual job evaluation, along with a 12 percent raise.

August: Will speak for our branch at the company's annual sales meeting in Newport.

September: Will receive my professional certification, as well as positive feedback about the proposal to split the department in two.

October: Will volunteer for a tour of duty as orientation director for new employees in the department. Will begin conducting one or two orientation sessions a month.

November: Will submit, on request, further information on the plan to split the department. Will celebrate my fifth anniversary with the company.

December: Will submit two newsletter articles on the profession to a national association.

Obviously, this projected list is a "living" document that requires continual revision as achievements occur. It is important to revise along the lines of goals and steps to achieve them, rather than just along the lines of what you know for sure will happen. In this way, you will be in charge of a logical pattern of accomplishments, and it will be more likely that they will bear a concrete relationship to your own goals.

Part **V**_____

Professional Exposure: Your World Ticket

Chapter 15 _____

Speaking Your Way to the Top

He who seizes the right moment is the right man.

Goethe

Here is a simple fact of career marketing. Professionals who speak well in public are more likely to be promoted than those who can't. Also, speaking in public can provide you with many new business contacts and possible additional income.

This chapter covers the two main areas of concern for anyone who wishes to enter the world of public speaking—what to talk about and how to get invited to speak.

YOUR SPEECH—WHAT ABOUT, HOW TO GIVE IT

Have you ever had an experience that is so unusual, or at least, so interesting, that you just had to share it? That is probably the best place to start. Another is to develop an expertise in an up-and-coming subject area. If you can accept the challenge of communicating abstract ideas through practical examples, you may be a good candidate for public speaking.

I can vividly recall the first time I ever spoke to a group professionally. It was in May 1976, and I was speaking to about 75 entrepreneurs at the Hartford District Office of the Small Business Administration. At the time I was working for a management consulting firm that provided marketing and management assistance to small- to medium-size businesses. One of our marketing activities to gain exposure for the firm was to serve as seminar leaders at SBA-sponsored workshops.

Although I had only been with the company six months, this Tuesday in May was to be my public speaking initiation. The presentation was 30 minutes long. I was very prepared and very qualified, having offered the same type of advice to individuals on a one-to-one level for two years.

When I got in front of the group, everything changed. The words were coming out and what I was saying had impact, but internally my stomach was doing somersaults. By the end of the session, a feather, literally, could have knocked me over; I was lightheaded, dizzy, exhilarated, and glad it was over.

In the months that followed, the presentation became easier and easier to give. I think it was finally after the sixth time that the butterflies left and my feet were firmly planted. And a funny thing happened by 1977—I actually started looking forward to speaking before groups. All of the things that I had read about the nervous energy that never dissipates didn't seem personally to apply. In succeeding years I was better prepared to communicate on the job, impressed bosses and coworkers with the names of groups I had spoken to, and began to acquire confidence that spilled over into other areas of my career.

You may never have considered speaking in public, yet becoming a good public speaker can help you to advance your career rapidly. Not only will you be perceived as bold and dynamic, but you will also gain visibility and new business contacts or clients.

Preparing to Speak

"The surest way to turn off an audience is to read a speech," says Maggie Bedrosian, author of *Speak Like a Pro.* People came to hear you speak, not to hear you read. Your first step in preparing your speech is to focus in on exactly what you want your speech to say to the group. Try describing the impact you want in just one sentence.

Then tackle two or three ideas at the most. It's far more effective to illustrate a few ideas substantially than to touch on a wide variety of topics. Examples and anecdotes will help your audience remember the main points.

You can't go wrong following the adage of the old Southern Baptist preacher: "Tell 'em what you're going to tell 'em, tell 'em, and then tell 'em what you told 'em."

A strong opening is vital to your audience's continued interest in your speech. If figures can document your point, use them. But be careful not to overwhelm your audience with figures throughout the speech. Members of the group will become disinterested if they hear too many numbers. The appropriate place for numbers and statistical data is in your handout.

Your conclusion is just as important. Make it dynamic, drawing together the points you have made in your speech with a strong example or anecdote.

After you've decided on your opening and closing, Bedrosian advises outlining the important parts of the body of the speech.

When outlining, use key words to remind you of the points to be made in that section. Writing out whole sentences will probably just distract you.

Practice your speech using the outline, written on notecards or any other method that is comfortable for you. Your speech will be different each time you practice it. Don't worry about that. It will be different also for each different audience to whom you give it. That is the secret of becoming a good public speaker—the ability to turn a speech, even to a huge audience, into a two-way conversation. You will modify your speech based on the energy level, intellectual understanding, enthusiasm, and myriad other factors about the audience.

Use the active voice at all times during your speech. If you use an unfamiliar or a technical word that your audience may not know, rephrase it or define it in the next sentence without being condescending.

Delivery Tips

Believe in your message and its importance to your audience. Lou Hampton, a professional speaker who has trained members of Congress, says "Become interested enough in your audience that your prime concern is how to get your message from you to them. When you think more about how you are going to put your message across and less about what people will think of you, you will end up a better communicator. So allow yourself to release your energy in a positive way."

Maggie Bedrosian advocates applying the "iceberg" formula to keep an audience interested. She describes great speakers as those who have a broad-based knowledge of their field but exhibit power by suggesting much greater knowledge kept out of sight.

"Such a speaker leaves most audiences hungering for more. And this is just as it should be. A 'hungry' audience will be moved to action. They are more inclined to explore further to seek results. A 'satisfied' group, on the other hand, may walk away thinking, 'Oh, that's nice. I wonder what's on the late show tonight,' " relates Bedrosian. Remember that the point of your presentation is "to stimulate the group into action, not satisfy them into complacency."

The Fine Points

If you find that you must use notecards, place them on the podium or table from which you will be speaking. However, move away from the podium whenever possible. A speaker who is moving seems more dynamic and involved, even if he or she were to use exactly the same words as a speaker frozen behind the lectern. Furniture only separates you from your audience. Once you get comfortable, step out from behind it; eventually, you will wonder why you ever needed it in the first place.

Your intonation is also important. Vary your pitch, tone, and speech according to the emphasis on your content. Tape one or two of your practice sessions to help you judge how you sound to an audience. (See Figure 15–1 for how judges view speakers.)

Paul Mills, president of Mills-Roberts Associates in New York, believes that most people speak several tones too high. The reason—they don't hear their voices as others do. "The sound reaches them through the head rather than through vibrations in the air, distorting the tone." Mills advises to speak low and use lots of jaw and lip movement. "This will improve tone, make you look more animated, and slow your delivery, giving you more time to think of what you want to say."

Hampton recalled a corporate president with whom he worked. "During the training session, he did a run-through of a presentation he was going to give at the annual stockholders meeting. It had been an extremely good year for the company. Sales and profits had increased dramatically. When we replayed the video tape, I turned to the president and said, 'Well, Tom, what do you think?' He said, 'Based on how I look and my tone of voice, they'll think we had a rotten year!' "

Figure 15–1. Judging the fine points.

A SPEAKING CHECKLIST

The following items are important in impromptu speeches:

Content Ideas, reception, description, logic.
Relevance Relation to topic, answer to question.
Speech Development Organization, thought, continuity.
Speech Structure Opening, body, closing.
Language Pronunciation, grammar, appropriateness.
Manner Assurance, directness, enthusiasm.
Voice Volume, pitch, use, flexibility.
Physical Gestures, movement, poise.

Here are important components for humorous speeches:

Speech Development Structure, opening, body, closing, organization, support material.
Effectiveness Excitement created, suspense, the unexpected twist, surprise, connection of humorous events, achievement of purpose.
Image Appearance, body language.
Originality Ideas, novelty of thought and material.
Audience Response Attentiveness, laughter, interest, reception.

Allow yourself to be expressive and natural in illustrating your points. "Most of us," says Hampton, "gesture when we're speaking one-on-one, but we clam up in front of a group." Do what you would do in conversation.

Occasionally, someone will insist that he or she just doesn't gesture. "One corporate executive we worked with was particularly adamant that he didn't gesture. The training session was interrupted by a call from his corporate headquarters. A division vice president needed an answer on some national advertising being planned," recalled Hampton. "We stopped the training session for half an hour while the client and his top assistants held a meeting. While discussing the situation, our client was leaning back in his chair, gesturing with large, expressive, smooth movements. Gesturing was natural for him, as it is for most people. I carefully observed each of his gestures and then immediately conveyed what I had observed. We reconvened our training session, and his reluctance to gesture had vanished."

Eye Contact

Closely related to the ability to allow your energy to come forth is the quiet skill of prolonged eye contact. This involves maintaining eye contact with an individual for three, four, or five seconds, or until you have completed a thought. Most speakers look at people momentarily before moving to someone else, scanning the audience rather than establishing specific eye contact. Don't let yourself slide into this bad habit.

It is important to establish eye contact, first, because it helps to reduce your tension. Second, by focusing on just one person, you can remind yourself that you are in a conversation. The fact that there may be 500 people in the room does not change the fact that everyone you speak to is interpreting you individually and will respond to you individually. If you look at somebody for three to five seconds, you have time really to see that individual. That will enable you to read the whole audience. You'll know, or sense, how they're responding.

Written Record

It always makes good sense to hand out something written with your presentation. If you distribute article reprints or other written material at the speaking engagement, you will at least make sure your audience leaves with your correct name and address. It also gives them something tangible with which to remember you. Frequently, I used an audience questionnaire, distributed at the outset, to quickly gauge what listeners came to hear (see the example in Figure 15–2).

You may enter the world of speech making with the idea of advancing your career or gaining new business, but never turn your speech into a direct attempt to self-promote or to make a sales pitch or sales presentation. Just speak on a topic of interest and do your best. Anything else is a turnoff and can backfire.

Few speeches or presentations bring instant results. One professional services consulting firm reports that it has received telephone calls from targets who heard a member of the firm speak several years previously.

Your decision on whether to seek speaking engagements as a personal promotional tool hinges on your ability to be interesting and to have something worthwhile to say to a group composed of targets of opportunity or influence. If you have never spoken before a group, you have a unique experience in store. Everyone is nervous at first, but, after a while you may find public speaking to be quite exhilarating.

HOW TO GET STARTED

Between mid-1982 and mid-1983, I spoke to more than 40 local groups while employed full time. My strategy for getting invited was simple. Each week I opened my local paper to the section on professional meetings. I called all the meeting planners listed and suggested that their members might benefit from my presentation. Often I did this for no fee. My compensation was developing my speaking skills, gaining exposure within the professional community, and converting tape transcripts into articles for publication. Subsequently I developed a brief flyer, which accelerated the number of requests (see Figure 15–3).

One way to spread the word on your availability for seminar presentations is to type a one-page letter explaining a little about
(continued on p. 163)

Figure 15–2. Audience questionnaire.

JPD

Jeffrey P. Davidson, CMC ▪ 3709 South George Mason Drive. #315E ▪ Falls Church. Virginia 22041 ▪ (703) 931-1984

DATE _____NAME OF WORKSHOP _____

NAME _____

MAILING ADDRESS _____

_____

TITLE AT WORK _____

ORGANIZATION/AGENCY _____

_____

_____

PHONE _____ (o) _____ (h)

If your wildest dreams come true, what will you learn in this workshop?

What is the *minimum* you must learn tonight in order to leave feeling satisfied?

_____

Figure 15–3. Public speaking flyer.

JEFF DAVIDSON, CMC

Can help you to:
- Manage Effectively in the 80's
- Win with Information
- Identify Lucrative Markets
- Get Ahead and Stay Ahead
- Sell Sell Sell

Credentials
Consulting

Certified Management Consultant (CMC) designation. Eight years, 180 clients in government and business; Marketing and MBA degrees.

Writing

250 articles published. Credits: Washington Post, Executive Review, Inc., Toastmaster, Rotarian, Washington Business Review, Office, more.

Award Winner: Small Business Administration "Media Advocate of the Year," "Outstanding Young Men in America."

Affiliation:

Institute of Management Consultants
National Speakers Association
Washington Independent Writers
Active Corps of Executives

Speaking
Engagements:

National Electrical Contractors
National League of American Pen Women
Independent Agents of Michigan
Washington Independent Writers
D.C. Chapter American Bar

Frequently Requested Topics:	• Getting Published Fast • Preparing the Marketing Plan • Promoting Your Cause • Finding Information • Light and Lively Management • Starting a New Venture
Address:	3709 S. George Mason Dr, 315E Falls Church, VA 22041
Telephone:	(703) 931-1984

your background. Also include a short paragraph description of three to five topics on which you are prepared to speak. You might say something like "my most frequently requested topics are: starting your own business, recordkeeping aspects of managing your own business, standing up to the IRS, developing a management style, and common mistakes of successful business professionals," or whatever topics on which you feel prepared to speak. List only those topics on which you can speak quite comfortably and on which you could conceivably answer questions from the audience, even if that is not a planned part of the presentation.

Your letter can be photocopied and distributed to perhaps as many as 50 groups in your local area. As a result of this one mailing, and depending on how well you are known in the community, you could generate two to five speaking engagements. For this or any other mailing, it is wise to send a second letter or to have someone on your staff make a follow-up telephone call.

Many local civic and charitable associations actively seek speakers. Yet, the program directors of these groups often must scramble to find an interesting speaker. Check your local newspaper as I did for the calendar of events that will list seminars offered by local organizations. You will probably be surprised by the number and variety of meetings in even the smallest community. Also, identify any local adult education programs. I polished my presentations for eight years with a Washington, D.C., outfit, offering as many as eight different seminars.

The best way to position yourself to be invited to speak to a local organization is to be a member of that group. But whether you're a member or not, be sure to contact meeting planners at least twice. You can call first, then mail your materials, and make a follow-up telephone call to each organization receiving your letter. This reinforces your desire to speak before that group. Or, you can simply mail first and then call. Personally, I find the first sequence to be more effective.

When some speech requests start arriving, you will need additional information from the group or groups before preparing your speech. To increase the effectiveness of your presentation, find out the size of the room, the setup (rows of seats, small tables, some other arrangement?), the expected attendance, the program length, the names and subject areas of any other speakers, the available sound system and audiovisual equipment, and the usual temperature and lighting in the speaking room (see the checklist example in Figure 15–4).

Be sure to ask whether you are responsible for running the audiovisual equipment. If you're not convinced of the importance of such details, try to remember the message of the last speaker you heard while sitting in a 90-degree room! Or, remember how you felt in front of an audience with your slides neatly arranged in a carousel, faced with an old box cartridge projector.

Supportive Speaking Organizations

To further your speaking capabilities, there are two excellent organizations you may wish to join.

The National Speakers Association is the professional association for public speakers. As a member you receive inside information and the opportunity to network with and learn from some of the top professional speakers in the world today. This is a

Figure 15–4. Speaking engagement checklist.

Meeting place

Size of room _____

Setup _____

Seating capacity _____

Sound system _____

Audiovisuals _____

Temperature/ventilation _____

Surrounding rooms _____

Comments _____

Audience Profile

Ages _____

Male/Female mix _____

Educational level _____

Professional experience (years) _____

Goals _____

Obstacles _____

Job description _____

Number of attendees _____

Comments _____

warm and friendly group, and practically everyone is willing to share information with you. The National Speakers Association has local chapters across the country. Psychologist Harry Olson says, "Here's where the action is year round. Ongoing programs to develop your skills, networking with local, friendly, professional speakers and business people like yourself, and new opportunities—all are yours at the local chapter level." NSA has over 30 chapters. Your local chapter will welcome your interest. For more details, contact the association at 4747 N. 7th Street, Suite 310, Phoenix, AZ 88014, (602) 265-1001.

Also contact your local Toastmasters chapter. Toastmasters is a worldwide organization with thousands of local chapters, which provide training in speaking skills. Olson observes that "NSA and Toastmasters often approach different aspects of speaking. Their programs are complementary, however, and many aspiring speakers belong to both. In NSA you will discover the aspects of speaking professionally. Toastmasters is more nuts-and-bolts speaking skills with feedback and evaluation." Toastmasters chapters can be found within large corporations for their employees, but they also exist independently and are open to the public. For a chapter near you, contact Toastmasters International, 2200 N. Grand Avenue, P.O. Box 10400, Santa Ana, CA 92711 (714) 542-6793.

Keep the following points in mind when using presentation and public speaking to aid in marketing your career:

- Become a member of local organizations; this is a good way to get invited to give presentations.
- Make your subject areas and availability known to other groups in your area.
- Analyze your audience carefully before preparing your speech.
- Write your speech in outline form, giving it a strong introduction and conclusion.
- Cover no more than three main points in any speech; use plenty of examples and anecdotes.
- Be aware of how your body language and vocal characteristics affect your presentation.
- Believe in your message and its importance to your audience.
- Practice; this will make you a better, more relaxed speaker.
- Join the National Speakers Association and Toastmasters.

Just how far can being a good speaker take you? Who knows? Perhaps as far as it has presently taken New York Governor Mario Cuomo. Largely as a result of his rousing speech at the 1984 Democratic Convention, he became acknowledged as a leading candidate for president of the United States.

Chapter **16**

Networking and Joining on Purpose

It is not enough to be busy, the question is what are we busy about?

Henry David Thoreau

Both networking and purposely joining certain groups and organizations can be important factors in your career marketing. Networking is a "buzz word" that struck the American business media full force in 1983. But its concept—making potentially useful contacts and building relationships with individuals, groups, and organizations—has been, and remains, an integral factor in business. And there is a true business magic in joining professional, civic, charitable, and social groups that is difficult

167

to describe. Let's consider each of these aspects of your career
marketing efforts.

NETWORKING

I prefer to use the term "focused networking" because I find
that too many people believe that networking means interacting
with everyone and anyone with whom they come in contact. Not
so. The truth is that whatever your field, whatever your profession, there are probably only ten to 20 key people that you must
know and influence in order to accelerate your career marketing
efforts.

Who are these key people? The surprising answer is that you
already know who they are. In my case they are other authors,
publishers, agents, and media people. For you, the answer may
be a few colleagues, several editors of industry publications, the
directors of professional associations in your industry, a couple
of leading businesspeople from your community, a career counselor, a mentor, and perhaps someone in another department of
your company.

Networking should be an ongoing part of a professional's
life. It serves many functions, including job search, accelerated
career climb, and professional fellowship. Those with an ingrained sense of career marketing recognize that what you
learn and the contacts you make outside the job help to advance
your career. Why? Because at the same time that you are constantly being exposed to new ideas, new people, new thoughts,
and new ways of looking at things, you are increasing *your*
exposure.

A large component of your career success is based on other
people. Certainly you have to be proficient in what you do. However, as a total "package," you must continuously be improving,
communicative, and forward-thinking. The business "woods" are

full of highly competent, well-trained, dedicated professionals
who do their jobs but never advance because they lack that well-
rounded "human" component that their bosses need to see for
promotion. Networking (and also joining associations) is a process
to be maintained whether you are looking for a new job or to
advance within your company.

What are the important components in networking? How can
networking benefit you?

What is Networking?

Networking can be as simple as a telephone call to a person
you worked with years ago, or as complex as analyzing several
trade associations most beneficial to your career advancement. It
is a continual process of sharing, passing along, and receiving
information that can help with your personal or business advancement.

Talk to everyone you can at professional meetings and gath-
erings. Later, make notes on the back of each card of conversation points that will help the person remember you. For example,
if you decide to follow up, say: "Hi, we met at the Cosmos Club
and talked about foreign hi-tech markets." Depending on the
number of cards you collect, go through them weekly or monthly
to weed them out.

Questions you may ask yourself when deciding which contacts to follow up include:

Do I like that person?
Did I feel challenged, excited by my conversation with that
    person?
Does that person have a high energy level?
Does that person have knowledge I need or want?
Does that person have contacts in my field?
Could that person advance my career at some time?
Could I help that person with his or her career?

Be selective. You can't be effective with an overly extended network.

Effective Components

According to Lee Gardenswartz and Anita Rowe, partners in Training and Consulting Associates, an effective network is composed of two different kinds of supporters: maintainers and propellers. Maintainers are those who help you get your job done competently and effectively; propellers push you into new areas to promote your advancement.

Gardenswartz and Rowe recommend use of the chart shown in Figure 16–1 to help you examine your network and where improvements in it could be made. To use the chart effectively, write in the names of people in your network who fit into each category in the left column. Next, in the right column, fill in the names, where possible, of people whom you *would like* as part of your network in those categories. Where you don't know a specific person, identify someone who can direct you in your search.

Formal Networking

Tomorrow's Business Leader says that networking is "just an 'in' word for association." Networking is people getting together to accomplish a particular purpose, and that's what associations have been since time immemorial. Formal networking is more direct than the informal networking discussed so far, and a major purpose of trade associations and professional groups is information-sharing and networking.

It is useful to join a professional organization, not only in your current field, but in the profession you want to join. If you're not sure which career path to take, you will get a good idea of what

Figure 16–1. Effective networking chart.

Maintainers

	Present	Future

KEYSTONES—People who form the core of your network -and are fundamental to getting your job done (e.g., an administrative assistant).

EXPERTS—Although these people do not propel your career, they are people in your field whom you respect and value as professional contacts and would recommend to others; those on whose professional competence you would stake your reputation.

TANGENTIAL HELPERS—People in related fields who help you get your job done (e.g., a writer needs an editor, publisher, and a graphic designer).

Propellers

	Present	Future

MENTORS—People who guide your career, provide opportunity and access, and teach you the ropes (see Chapter 4).

ROLE MODELS—People whose professional behavior stimulates ideas for your future. They have achieved what you aspire to; they are examples to emulate.

HUBS—Those who refer you to additional sources of information and people. They suggest helpful connections.

CHALLENGERS—People who cause you to look at your own direction, force you to face some important questions about your own life.

PROMOTERS/RECOMMENDERS—People who advise you of opportunities and encourage your visibility.

the field involves by joining an association of its members (see Joining on Purpose later in this chapter).

Establishing Networking Goals

The following list offers examples of what could be your personal networking goals:

- Meet one new person in my profession each week.
- Attend two major professional conventions this year.
- Write to five leading authors by the end of the month.
- Join two new local organizations comprised of community business leaders.
- Call all 168 people on my rolodex in the next three months (an average of only two per day).
- Obtain a directory of professionals in my field and become familiar with those who are residents of my state.
- Attend three mixers as a prospective member of a group, such as Chamber of Commerce, the Board of Trade, and the United Way.

In as little as six months, you may find that you have completely revitalized your address book or rolodex. People open doors for you, and by undertaking focused networking, you can make contact with just the right "keys."

Networking can be useful if you remember to keep it focused, weeding out contacts periodically, and recognize that it is a continual process of sharing information and favors.

JOINING ON PURPOSE

During my fifth year in the working world, I joined Washington Independent Writers because it was becoming obvious that I liked to write. The number of articles that I was writing after work and on weekends led me to believe that someday I might have a future in writing. Two years later, I joined another professional group specifically to increase my exposure and professionalism. During the summer of 1982, Jefferson D. Bates, author of *Writing With Precision, Dictating Effectively*, and *Take Your Office on the Road*, invited me to a monthly meeting of National Capital Speakers Association, the Washington, D.C., regional chapter of the National Speakers Association.

At my first meeting I experienced personal revelation. Here I met for the first time people who were highly enthusiastic and who had important messages to offer. Some of them delivered seminars and training sessions locally; others spoke across the country on a full-time basis, and for very healthy fees. Being the youngest at this meeting, you can imagine what solid, eye-opening contacts awaited.

Today I still belong to that association and my membership has paid off handsomely. I have since joined the American Marketing Association, the Greater Washington Society of Association Executives (although I am not an association executive), and the Institute of Management Consultants.

The magic that takes place when you join professional, civic, charitable, and social groups is, indeed, hard to describe. When you join these types of organizations, you are rubbing elbows with the winners in society. If you were to travel across the country, stopping in any city, you could readily find the most prosperous people in the community by simply heading toward the hotels, restaurants, convention centers—any place where there are meeting rooms. Read the marquee to see who is in attendance, go up to the registration table, and tell them you would like to learn more about that group.

You might ask what *specific* benefits I received as a result of my various memberships. My membership in Washington Independent Writers enabled me to meet other authors throughout the region. Many offered valuable tips on getting an agent, getting an advance for books, preparing manuscript proposals, and assisting the publisher with marketing once the book is published. As a result of joining the National Capital Speakers Association, I raised my speaking fee in that year alone from $185 to $480. I subsequently raised it again to $750, and then to $1,200. When I first joined National Capital Speakers, I didn't believe anybody in the world could get more than a couple of hundred dollars for a speaking engagement. But befriending and networking with people who regularly did it was all the evidence I needed. These, of course, are only two examples of specific benefits I received from networking.

I was particularly fortunate to be among the youngest in all the groups that I joined. It is fine and rewarding to be with your own age group, but for accelerated career advancement, I recommend meeting with those who are five, ten, and even many more years senior.

Join and Serve

Business leaders know that giving their time freely is an excellent way to be of service to the community and to help develop a solid professional and personal reputation. The opportunity to interact with key community and business leaders, to work jointly on solving local problems are other key benefits of joining such organizations. While you are gaining personal exposure, others in the group will assume that you are fully competent in your profession and a rising star in the community.

Earning a position of leadership in a high visibility organization is an excellent way to be of service and, as a by-product, enhance your career potential. By volunteering your services and assisting civic and charitable organizations, targets of opportunity—those who may provide your next job—come to know you as a person and can then feel comfortable discussing business opportunities and problems with you.

Your organizational skills will become evident in the course of your association with a group. Do you volunteer for committee activities? Do you deliver what you promise? Can you handle leadership within the group? Affirmative answers to these questions could get the attention of someone who could advance your career.

Selective Joining

Any local group tends to be run by small cliques. The lead time necessary to break into these subgroups and begin receiving benefits from the organization can range anywhere from six to 18 months. Many professionals don't stand their ground. They drop out and never realize that the benefits of being known and accepted in the group were "just around the corner."

Despite the advantages, joining professional and civic groups can be a drain on your time and energy if you are not selective. Evaluate your memberships in these groups to determine:

- If you are meeting and working with people who could help in your career advancement.
- If you are personally satisfied with the work the group is doing.
- If you like the people in the organization.
- If the long-term benefits will equal the energy and time you spend.

Each community is somewhat different and the interplay of political, social, cultural, and religious spheres varies, so some thought must be given as to what groups to join and why. Continually analyze local organizational contacts for relationships that should be developed, paying particular attention to senior executives and entrepreneurs who may be expanding operations. This approach must be balanced, however, with the realization that the only organizations you should join are those in which you have a genuine interest and desire to serve. Purely Machiavellian aims seldom pay off and can cause resentment among others in the organization.

National and Local Organizations

The following list includes national as well as local organizations that are likely to have chapters in your area. Check your local telephone book for the address of any group that interests you and call for membership information.

Active Corps of Executives	Jaycees
American Business Women's	Kiwanis
Association	League of Women Voters
American Cancer Society	Lions
American Heart Association	March of Dimes
American Legion	Masons
American Marketing Association	National Association of
Boys' Club	Professional Saleswomen
B'nai Brith	Optimists Club
Catholic Youth Organization	Parent-Teacher Association
Civitans	Public Television
Democratic party	Republican party
Easter Seal Campaign	Rotary Club
Elks	Sales Executives International
Explorers	Salvation Army
Garden clubs	Scouts of America
Goodwill Industries	Society of Association Executives
Heart Fund	Toastmasters
Historical Society	United Way
Independent party	Urban League
International Association of	YMCA, YWCA
Business Communicators	

Getting the Most Out of Joining

Join committees.

The work of the organization is done in committees. They usually have very specific tasks, meeting more often than the general membership and offering more of a chance for the camaraderie that becomes natural in small group work. A position such as activities chair gives you high visibility and virtually unlimited access to key people in your market area. The membership committee or social committee can also be a high visibility position.

Be realistic.

Although it's important to volunteer for committee activities, take on only what you can realistically accomplish. Nothing turns off a group more quickly than a promise that isn't kept. Excuses, no matter how good they seem to you, will fall flat to a group that has counted on your work.

Follow up.

If Joe Smith tells you he would be interested in your ideas on a business problem you discussed over coffee at the last United Way meeting, follow up quickly and professionally. Some people maintain card files on individuals when a key contact is made. Information is continually added to the card file.

Don't flaunt it.

Membership in a civic organization should not be waved like a flag. Quiet, subtle references will ensure that your commitment to the group will be noticed. Every once in a while, do something on behalf of the organization without mentioning it.

Check Appendix A for a list of some of the professional organizations you may want to consider joining as a first step in your networking process.

You can gain a measure of visibility by joining key civic organizations in your community. But remember that the cycle for getting known and accepted in the group may range from six to

18 months. You must constantly monitor and analyze your memberships to make sure you are getting a good return for the time invested, at the same time joining only groups in which you have a genuine interest and desire to serve.

Finally, you must meet, and be remembered by, those with whom you network and targets of opportunity for effective career marketing.

Chapter 17

Breaking into Print

Success teaches me the necessity of patience.

Sri Chinmoy

In 1976, as an employee of a small consulting firm in Connecticut, I approached my boss during a slow period in the work week and asked what I might do to help the firm during this time. He suggested writing an article, an activity that would *never* have occurred to me, a B- student in English composition with no writing aspirations.

After several false starts, I hit upon a simple formula to help me through my first piece. The title of the article was "Ten Tips on Survival for Small Business." The concept was simple. I would come up with 10 different tips that would be the start of a paragraph or perhaps a couple of paragraphs. I would then add an opening paragraph and a closing paragraph, and that would be my whole article. This article was particularly easy to write. As

I later found, whenever you attach a number to your title, such as "Eight Ways" to do something better, you instinctively finish the article without struggling, even if you don't perhaps reach eight ways (you might only reach six).

We first mailed my manuscript out to a publication that sat on it for five months and then rejected it. We then mailed to another publication, *The New Englander*, which sat on it for four months. Then one day, without advance notice or word of any kind, a package arrived. It was thick. I opened it and found that my article, "Ten Tips on Survival for Small Business," was published in the October 1976 issue of *The New Englander* magazine. As it turned out, it was the last article in the issue—the least of my concerns. The graphics and artwork that they had done were wonderful and the article made an extremely attractive reprint. I was so excited to have my name in print that I must have photocopied that article 500 times and sent it to everyone I knew.

Although the magazine paid me nothing, the lesson I learned was priceless. Up until that time I thought that only superstars and the privileged classes ever got their name in print. By October 1979, when I discovered portable dictation equipment, I began dictating articles at the pace of about one a month, increasing within a year to one per week.

Benefits of Publishing

It is important to have realistic expectations of what publishing can do for you. Publishing articles in newspapers and magazines can greatly accelerate career marketing efforts and offer a sense of pride in the accomplishment. Publishing will probably not put you on the best-seller list or get you on the Johnny Carson show. However, all other things being equal, if you have had a couple of articles published, you are better positioned for advancement than a coworker who has not. Note the benefits:

Establishes credentials.

Getting published means credentials for you in the article topic area. If a supervisor in an engineering firm, for example, writes an article on reinforcing bridge supports, a public notice has been made that he or she, and the firm, have expertise in this area. A firm requiring a subcontractor on a bridge design project may call the writer's firm merely on the basis of the article.

Builds editor/publisher relationships.

Especially if you concentrate on one subject area, you are likely to gain ever-wider acceptance with magazines in your field and can better keep abreast of new developments while increasing your visibility.

Supplies article reprints.

You can create a favorable impression by supplying clients, coworkers, and associates with reprints of an article you have had published. Modesty aside, most authors are very proud of their work and have no qualms about submitting reprints to friends, relatives, and associates. Many people are pleased and impressed to accept your reprint. Naturally, you should use this technique discreetly and with judgment to avoid appearing boastful or egotistical.

Bolsters marketing efforts.

For instance, you can include reprints of your article with résumés when applying for a new position and with raise requests on your present job.

Invites speaking invitations.

An article may result in an invitation to speak before a particular group. Every article can be made into a speech, and vice versa. Giving speeches will put you in touch with others interested in your subject area, who will likely know other places to publish your articles. This circular exchange of information can prove very beneficial.

Spotlights your name and company.

Your company's name should always be mentioned in your biography when you write an article. For example, "Joe Smith is a manager with XYZ Corporation." Your article will, therefore, market both you and your firm. If possible, without stretching the content, you may want to mention your company's name in the body of the article. (Use caution, however, with this technique. Some companies are sensitive about publicity and would prefer *not* to be mentioned in connection with an employee's activities. Understand your company's unwritten rules in this area before going ahead.)

The benefits of getting published may continue for a surprisingly long time. A friend of mine got a letter about an article he had published in a monthly trade magazine two-and-a-half years before. But this is not unusual. Your article may live on as long as there are libraries.

Where to Publish

The number of general, industrial, business, professional, and in-house publications has risen dramatically since the early 1970s. First, try your own company in-house newsletter if you are in a large organization, or the in-house publications of companies in your field. The personnel or human resources department will usually be responsible for the newsletter's publication, or will know who is.

You can obtain the name, address, telephone number, editorial content, fees paid, circulation, target audience, and submission requirements for more than 10,000 journal magazines by checking one of the following directories in the reference section of your library:

Bacon's Publicity Checker.
Magazine Industry Marketplace.
Working Press of the Nation.
Writer's Market.
Ayer's Directory of Publications.
Gebbie's All in One Directory.

To help you get started, the names and addresses of dozens of business, management, and career-related magazines and journals are listed in Appendix B.

Finding Topics

The best topics for articles are derived from the *successful work that you have already done*. This includes reports, papers, summaries, guides, and exhibits that you have prepared, perhaps for work, which can be generalized and applied to a larger audience. Even if you have never written about a subject, you may have an article inside you if you have special knowledge or insights.

Following are some ways to generate article topics and start on the route to getting published.

Begin a clip file.

Every time you read the Sunday newspaper or a professional journal, save articles that interest you or strike your fancy. You may not even know how you would use the article at this time.

File all of the clippings by topic or subject area. Months later, review your clip file, and you will find that what you've clipped serves as the catalyst for numerous article ideas. Freelance writers have successfully used the clip file technique for years.

Develop a "how to" list.

Think of six, eight, or more ways to do something better. The market for "how to" articles has for years been increasing steadily as more and more people thirst for "do-it-yourself" information. By introducing a number into the title of your article, such as "Seven Ways to Accomplish XYZ," you have established a hook that will attract readers.

Make a gripes list.

A list of gripes or discomforts in connection with your place of work can contain the seeds of articles. If something bothers you, it undoubtedly bothers others. Discuss the problem in broad terms and offer suggestions for redress. By recognizing the universality of a problem that you face, you will be creating material for an excellent article.

Recall a person or experience.

An unforgettable staff member (or boss), a favorite professional experience, your biggest disappointment, or other memorable event can point up some underlying lesson, something we can all use in our reading material.

Identify the target audience.

If you can concentrate for a moment on who will be reading your article and what impact it will have on them, the task of completing your writing will flow more smoothly. Think of the last time you wrote a letter to a friend or relative and how easily the words and ideas came. Your writing task was on a one-to-one basis and your target audience was perfectly defined. You can achieve the same effect when you precisely define the target group that will be reading your article. If it's helpful to you, write the name of your target group on the top of your outline, such as "peers," "project staff," "executives earning over $80,000 per year."

Don't write.

Or, at least don't write an article from scratch. Perhaps the best single tip I can offer is to review all of the reports, proposals, papers, memos, outlines, and such that you have ever written and saved to determine their applicability as articles. As a management consultant, at the end of each engagement I always had to write a client report. From those reports I frequently was able to pull out five- and six-page passages that could be generalized and applied to a larger audience. If you have saved your college papers, you might find one or two publishable articles from term papers and compositions that you submitted for a letter grade. You will be amazed to find that editors of publications are often much easier to deal with than your professors were. Also, remember that larger articles sometimes make wonderful shorter articles.

Produce spin-offs.

If you have already written one article, perhaps the greatest technique for generating other articles is to produce a spinoff. As an example, years ago I wrote an article entitled "How to Build a Law Practice," following a consulting engagement I had with a Washington, D.C., law firm. The article essentially followed a "14 tips" format although I didn't use that title. I sent the article to *Case and Comment* in Rochester, New York, which accepted it for

Figure 17–1. Generic article topics.

How to _____

_____*Reasons Why* _____

_____**Ways to Improve** _____

_____*to Consider Before* _____

_____**Pitfalls** _____

New Developments _____

A _____**Approach to** _____

The Art of _____

Overcoming Resistance to _____

Planning for Your _____

publication. About a year later I was going through my manuscript file and came across the article. It dawned on me that with
very little time and effort I could convert that article to "How to
Build a Medical Practice." In the previous year I had worked with
a couple of doctors and dentists and was now familiar with their
terminology and the differences required to restructure my earlier article. I subsequently rewrote "How to Build a Law Practice"
14 times, including versions for dentists, realtors, insurance
agents, accountants, psychiatrists, graphic artists, consultants, and
others. If selecting an article topic is difficult for you, or particularly if you suffer from writer's block, consider those articles
and those topics that lend themselves to spin-offs, and you will
find yourself doubling, tripling, and quadrupling your publishing
efforts.

Figure 17–1 shows 10 generic article topics, and Figure 17–2
shows how these topics were turned into potential articles.

Most people agree that having an article published is certainly
a worthwhile endeavor. At lectures and speaking engagements, I
have frequently pointed out that if you were to stop reading the

Figure 17–2. Potential articles.

How to Ask for a Bigger Office

Six Reasons Why Using a PC Will Decrease your Efficiency

Eight Ways to Improve Your Vocabulary

Items to Consider Before Changing Jobs

Four Pitfalls in Working for a Government Agency

New Developments in Laser Technology

A New Approach to Group Decision-Making

The Art of Closing the Sale

Overcoming Resistance to Reorganization

Planning for Your Next Job Promotion

Sunday paper just a few times every couple of months and instead devoted that time to writing an article, in the course of the year you could have three or four articles written and, perhaps, published. By the end of three or four years, you might have between six and ten articles published. This would put you in the upper one percent of the population in terms of being in print.

Overcoming Writer's Block

Writer's block hangs heavy over the head of many a career marketer. If writer's block is a problem for you, the following suggestions may help you to get started:

Create an outline of an idea.

Over the years, I've found that producing a one-page outline, or writing as little as ten key words on a page, was more than sufficient as guidance through the preparation and completion of an article. Devote a block of time simply to preparing article outlines or chronological sequences that can later serve as useful tools when you're ready to write the full-blown article.

Think of "published author."

Imagine how that phrase will look on your résumé. By visualizing the rewards of writing and getting your article published, you can break out of the chains that may currently restrain you and get started on an article that you can finish today.

Avoid extraneous reading.

Think of all the times that you read the Sunday newspaper and within three days forgot 95 percent of what you had read. Analyze what the continual reading of the newspaper has done for your income, career, and life in general, and you might agree that you could skip reading the newspaper now and then, write an article, and enjoy the benefits of getting published.

Clear your desk.

Get rid of everything except what's needed to write your article. People often have trouble writing because their desk is a mess and not conducive to creativity. Recognize that during the time you're preparing an article you must tune out distractions. An effective way to do this is to work on a clear surface.

Write for five minutes.

And see what happens. Forget all the excuses. Set an alarm, sit down, and start writing. Often you will find that you don't want to stop after five minutes. Getting started is the key obstacle to writing productively. If you can master the "five-minute technique," you will develop a habit that will blast the term "writer's block" out of your vocabulary. The five-minute technique is so effective that even if you cannot complete the article at the initial sitting, you undoubtedly will finish faster and more easily than you would have otherwise.

Publication and Your Career Marketing Program

A large part of the benefits you can expect from publication of an article depends on how you take advantage of it. I never count on the probability that my target market will see and remember the article when it is first published. It's nice when that happens, but the odds, unfortunately, are against it. It is more important to make an attractive, professionally produced reprint that can be leveraged in support of your career marketing efforts. Here are action steps you can take:

Mail reprints to your clients and associates.
Give copies to your peers, relatives, and friends.
Talk to the editor and/or publisher immediately to get ideas for further articles you could write for that publication.
Mention the article (and publication) in your telephone conversations.

How to Get in Others' Articles

If writing an article is good for your career advancement, think of the benefit that can come from being quoted as an expert by another writer. To do this, contact writers you respect with comments on their articles. Even criticism, if well thought out and useful, may be the basis of a professional relationship with professional writers covering your field. Once you have their respect, offer to send them material they can use in their columns. If you have something interesting to say, there is no reason why they won't use your name.

My good friend Robert Bookman lives in Arlington, Virginia,

and frequently reads the *Washington Post* "Style Plus" column. On several occasions he noticed that one of the staff writers, Don Oldenburg, wrote on topics that were of particular interest to him. My friend began a professional, aggressive letter-writing campaign to influence Don Oldenburg to write about Bookman's team productivity programs. Read Bookman's correspondence (Figure 17–3) to learn how to use this tactic with success.

In a matter of weeks a major article appeared in the *Washington Post* featuring Bookman's team productivity program. However, the story doesn't end there. A few weeks after the article appeared, my friend suggested that I get in touch with Don Oldenburg to do a story on me concerning the value of promoting yourself to get ahead in your career. Robert was nice enough to write Don Oldenburg to let him know that I would be making contact. I first called Don Oldenburg, followed up with a package of career marketing materials, and followed that up with another call.

Several months went by before I was finally interviewed. And several more weeks went by before the article was published. But on May 20, 1985, there it was, splashed across the Style Plus section of the *Washington Post*—an article entitled "Putting Your Best Self Forward," which reflected my 90-minute interview.

Oldenburg happened to be a member of the *Washington Post* Syndicated Writer's Group and, to make things better, the article appeared in hundreds of other papers across the country. Since the article prominently mentioned my first book, sales picked up nationally and, within its first year, the book was in its third printing.

Is my experience unique? Does it take any special gift to attain this kind of professional recognition and exposure? Not at all. A little creative thinking and some hard work can enable you to achieve the same sort of results for your own career marketing efforts.

Figure 17–3. Three steps to successful publicity.

Robert Bookman
President

December 27, 1984

Mr. Don Oldenburg
Style Plus
WASHINGTON POST
1150 15th Street
Washington, D.C. 20071

Dear Don:

As I mentioned to you over the phone today, I believe my work in the area of teamwork and team productivity will be of interest to your readers. I have conducted team productivity programs for some of this city's largest organizations (e.g., American Security Bank, Mitre, Wang Laboratories, U.S. Navy), and have found that the reasons work teams are productive or unproductive do not always show up on organizational charts or yearly reports.

Productivity often depends on people's ability to be able to withstand the hurts that go into mature conflict resolution. I have had the chief executive officer of a major D.C. corporation explain to me that he was reorganizing the corporation simply because he was afraid ("didn't think it appropriate") to confront a senior vice president. This C.E.O. was not only wasting time with unnecessary reorganizations, but was also creating corporate norms that would hinder team productivity. Healthy corporate norms (cooperation, trust, loyalty, participation) support people's ability to appropriately deal with the strains inherent in all cooperative efforts.

Over the past six years I have accumulated both useful information and amusing anecdotes on how productive teams operate. I think your readers can both benefit from and enjoy what I have learned. I hope to meet with you to further explore the possibility of having Style Plus do a story on my work. Perhaps you would like to hear one of my talks. In two weeks I will be giving a presentation entitled Teamwork: What Those Beer Commercials Don't Tell You! before the American Society of Personnel Administrators.

Could we possibly get together on January 7th, or January 8th?

Unless I hear from you earlier, I will give you a call on January 4th.

Wishing you a healthy and prosperous New Year,

Sincerely,

Robert Bookman

Figure 17–3, continued

Robert Bookman
President

January 3, 1985

Mr. Don Oldenburg
Style Plus
WASHINGTON POST
1150 15th Street
Washington, D.C. 20071

Dear Don:

After we spoke today, I started to think about the appeal an article on Team Productivity in STYLE PLUS would have for the general public. Naturally, I think an article on our society's present love affair with the word "team" would have broad appeal.

Our society is mesmerized by this word "team." There's Team Xerox, the NBC News Team, and America's Team—whether it be the Atlanta Braves or Dallas Cowboys. Why is today's vernacular "teaming" with the word team? One major reason is due to the success of Japan's workteam concept. This success is contributing to a shift in the high value we place on rugged individualism to—something else. This something else is often referred to as "teamwork." Yet most Americans (unlike most Japanese) are still uncomfortable with the team concept. Teams, unlike yesterday's officemates, are often short term and require enormous degrees of instant cooperation, trust, loyalty, keeping commitments, acceptance of others, and an "everybody can win attitude." Such qualities usually take quite a bit of time to develop. Yet today's work place is demanding that we quickly adhere to a new work style.

In essence, I'm suggesting that many people need to be changing their fundamental work style in order to be successful in today's work environment. A problem exists in that many organizations have not informed employees of the new team-oriented work behavior now expected, nor are employees being given the assistance in making those attitudinal and behaviorial changes necessary to conform to such norms. Ten years ago, the norm for getting ahead within most work settings was to "kick a little ass" (as George Bush would say), or to "butter up" the boss. Now the norm is—participate, cooperate, and facilitate the efforts of your fellow teammates. The concept of teamwork sounds easy, but for the majority of Americans, being a member of a team is hard work—damn hard work. The Team Productivity Programs that I deliver to major organizations in the D.C. area assist people in obtaining the skills that they need to become successful and well-adjusted team players.

I do hope we can "team up" to do an article. Unless I hear from you earlier, I'll give you a call this coming Tuesday, January 8th.

Sincerely,

Robert Bookman

Figure 17–3, *continued*

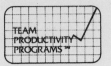

Robert Bookman
President

February 2, 1985

Mr. Don Oldenburg
Style Plus
WASHINGTON POST
1150 15th Street
Washington, D.C. 20071

Dear Don:

The instrument that I gave you indicates that your behavioral characteristics fall into the category of "Persuader." On page seventeen there's a short description of the "Persuader Pattern." A more complete description of this pattern is contained in the enclosed booklet titled: Library of Classical Patterns. Pages one through fourteen of the booklet are merely filler, so I suggest you start reading from page fifteen. Please let me know if you have any questions regarding this material or the instrument.

Don, you said there was a good possibility of having your readers be able to get in touch with me by making my telephone number available in the article. My other suggestion was using a photo. You thought that a plain photo of me really wouldn't add to the story, but possibly an "action shot" makes sense. With this possibility in mind, I had several action shots taken last week at a team productivity session I was leading of civilians working with the U.S. Navy. Now, I'm not suggesting you use ALL the photos(!), but perhaps. . . .

I think the article on my team productivity work can make an important impact on your readers. It can help them be more productive and less stressful on their job, it can help their organization be more profitable, and it can give employees and employers an understanding of what work styles are most appropriate for success. As you know, a most effective way to get folks to read such an important article is to have a photograph that catches the eye. Don, the instrument you took also categorizes me within the "Persuader Pattern," so how am I doing?

With or without a telephone number here, and a quack quack there, here a photo there a photo everywhere a . . . I wish to thank you for taking the time to consider my initial telephone call, and subsequently write an article on the work that I consider so important.

Looking forward to hearing when the article will appear.

All the best,

Robert Bookman

Chapter 18

Becoming Your Own Press Agent

Many a small thing has been made large by the right kind of advertising.

Mark Twain

What you do is news, perhaps not front page headline news, but every morning or evening, the local paper features brief news items about professionals in your community. These are often found on the business or financial pages, under town news, or elsewhere in sections such as "People to Watch" or "Names in the News." In Chapter 14, we discussed listing a year in advance all that you hoped to accomplish. Each item that makes your internal achievements list can also be prepared as a press or news release.

Consider for a moment the likely events that will take place in your coming year. You will probably attend a conference or two. You may have an article published, you may be giving a speech, you may be traveling abroad, you may be winning an award, undoubtedly you will be celebrating some type of anniversary, and you will probably get a raise or promotion. Some or all of these events may be considered newsworthy by your local media.

It is time to become your own press agent and begin to generate significant, positive exposure in the media. For strategic career marketers who are aiming for the top quickly realize that developing good relations in today's media-driven society is not optional. Begin now to tabulate the names and addresses of editors and reporters, both locally and nationally, who cover your industry.

Several directories in Appendix C list the names and addresses of newspapers, magazines, journals, and other periodicals. I maintain several media lists. One is a list of local reporters and publications to whom I send a press release approximately every three months. I have another list of editors of national publications in my industry. These include such publications as *Marketing News, Marketing Communications,* and the *Journal of Professional Service Management.* I also maintain lists of newsletter editors, book reviewers, and fellow authors. The common denominator to everyone on my list is that they can all potentially publish my press releases and articles, or mention me in some way.

But the newspaper is not the only game in town. Your own organization's in-house newspaper or newsletter, neighborhood and shoppers guides, church and synagogue bulletins, and local townhouse or condominium newsletters, as well as other publications, all are likely to accept your news releases. In many ways, the readership of these "smaller" publications can be of greater importance to you, depending on who reads them.

NEWS RELEASES

Figure 18–1 presents just a few of all the topics that are suitable for news releases. Start a clipping file of news releases submitted by others that catch your eye and you will be able to greatly expand this topic list.

Send and Be Silent

Once you have made contact with the editors of the various print media you have selected, send your news releases on a regular basis, perhaps monthly or quarterly. *Never* call the editor, seek a publication date, or ask for clippings. This is the quickest guarantee to getting your news releases filed in the trash. Editors are busy people, too, and can easily be irritated by those who call to ask about news or press releases. In the long run, your chances are much better if you simply write a good release and keep quiet. Dr. Michael Reagen offers several suggestions on increasing your chances of getting published:

- Use your first name, middle initial, last name, and title the first time you mention yourself in the release.
- Use a simple, straightforward style with average length sentences. (I recommend no more than 23 words per sentence.)
- Type the news release on clean 8 × 11 paper, placing your phone number in the upper left- or right-hand corner and instructions as to when to use the release in the opposite corner, for instance, "For immediate use" or "For use the week of September 3."
- If the release is more than one page (it is not recommended to go beyond two pages), put the word *more* on the bottom of the first page.
- Lead off with who, what, when, where, why, and how.
- Send along a picture, if possible.

Figure 18–1. Suitable topics for news releases.

Jeffrey P. Davidson, CMC ▪ 3709 South George Mason Drive. #315E ▪ Falls Church. Virginia 22041 ▪ (703) 931-1984

Your Professional Activities

Speaking engagements
Reprints of speeches
Travel abroad
Interesting backgrounds, hobbies
Noteworthy accomplishments
Appearance on radio or television
Civic activities
Elections, appointments
Courses completed, certificates, degrees
Seminars attended
Publications, books, articles
Mention in trade, professional journals
Awards, citations, honors

Your Services

New projects
Studies completed
Office expansion, renovation, relocation
New service introduction
New uses for existing products
Lower cost due to more efficient operation
Unusual service offerings
Bids or awards
New contracts

Your Firm

Affiliation
Accomplishments
Anniversaries of firm, principals, or long-term employees
Association memberships
New building or radical office change
Banquets or awards dinners
Employee training programs
Projected plans
Joint programs—government, industry

Research

Survey results
New discoveries
Trends, projections, forecasts

- Send to the particular department editor if it involves a special interest.
- Be accurate. If you are not, it might be your last chance.

The editors to whom you send your release will decide on using your story based on any local angle, the general news interest, the paper's policy, and timing. Figure 18–2 comprises two press releases of mine that were picked up by area press. I submitted the first, "Local Consultant Has First Book Published" to 15 local publications, and three of them carried my story. Remember that unless you scan the papers carefully, you might miss the publication of your own release. The second, "Author to Visit Soviet Union" was picked up by the Hartford Courant, a major Connecticut newspaper.

Taking Photos

I go to the photographer about once a year and get eight or ten different shots taken. Part of my strategy in gaining exposure and recognition is to continuously use different pictures on book jackets and magazine articles and in press releases. It's boring to see the same picture of someone used over and over for years.

When you hire a photographer to have your picture taken, there are several options. One is what is called the head and shoulder shot, which you will be able to use for virtually all of the types of promotional vehicles we have discussed. However, you may also wish to have action photos. An action photo might include you in front of a seminar group, receiving an award, or conferring with a colleague. Sometimes action photos can be staged in the photographer's studio, but often they have to be taken on the spot.

Another type of photo is what I call the candid shot, in which you are seated at your desk, or in some other familiar home-type or working environment that gives the reader a sense of your

(continued on p. 201)

Figure 18–2. Press releases that made the news.

Jeffrey P. Davidson, CMC ■ 3709 South George Mason Drive. #315E ■ Falls Church. Virginia 22041 ■ (703) 931-1984

For Immediate Release

For More Information
Contact: Jeff Davidson
931-1984

LOCAL CONSULTANT HAS FIRST BOOK PUBLISHED

Jeffrey P. Davidson, a certified management consultant from Falls Church, has co-authored a book which is being shipped this week to major book stores nationwide. The book is entitled *Marketing Your Consulting and Professional Services* and is published by John Wiley & Sons, 605 Third Avenue, New York, NY 10158.

Davidson is a frequent speaker at conventions and seminars offering a wide range of presentations on the management and marketing of professional service firms. As a Certified Management Consultant, a designation awarded by the Institute of Management Consultants, he has obtained the industry's high accreditation.

He has also authored numerous articles appearing in periodicals and journals such as *Private Practice, Case and Comment, Real Estate Today, Legal Economics, Dental Management, ABA Banking Journal, Business and Society Review, Professional Insurance Agent, National Public Accountant, Georgetown Law Weekly, Personnel Journal,* and many others.

Davidson has a degree in Marketing and an MBA, and is a designated Connecticut State Scholar. He is listed in *Who's Who in Finance and Industry* and *Outstanding Young Men of America.* Previously he was named the Washington, D.C. "Small Business Media Advocate of the Year", and an American Institute of Management "Executive of Distinction".

Figure 18–2, continued

Jeffrey P. Davidson, CMC ▪ 3709 South George Mason Drive. #315E ▪ Falls Church. Virginia 22041 ▪ (703) 931-1984

For Immediate Release   For More Information
                                                          Contact: Jeff Davidson
                                                                 931-1984

AUTHOR TO VISIT SOVIET UNION

Jeff Davidson will be visiting the Soviet Union this spring to examine problems of entrepreneurship in a state-controlled society. Jeff was recently named 1984 Washington, D.C. Small Business Media Advocate of the Year and is co-author of the forthcoming book *Marketing Your Consulting and Professional Services*, John Wiley & Sons, New York, publisher.

Jeff is a frequent speaker at conventions and seminars offering a wide range of presentations on the management and marketing of professional service firms. As a CMC (Certified Management Consultant awarded by the Institute of Management Consultants), he has obtained his industry's high accreditation.

Later this year Jeff will be addressing the D.C. Institute of CPA's, the Greater Washington Society of Association Executives, Northern Virginia Associated Builders & Contractors, National Rural Electric Co-operatives Association, and the D.C. Chapters of American Society of Women Accountants, the Project Management Institute, and other groups.

Jeff has become one of the nation's most prolific business authors. He has authored numerous articles appearing in periodicals and journals such as *Washington Post, Case and Comment, Real Estate Today, Legal Economics, Dental Management, ABA Banking Journal, Business and Society Review, Professional Insurance Agent, National Public Accountant, Executive Review, Georgetown Law Weekly, New Englander, Personnel Journal,* and hundreds of others.

He holds a BS in marketing and an MBA from the University of Connecticut.

surroundings. Some photographers are equipped to create this type of environment within the studio. Obviously, it is best to check in advance.

The News Release in Perspective

Only a small percentage of the news releases you send out will be published. However, the number of column inches that even one release generates, as opposed to paying for an ad, is really quite a bonanza. What exactly does getting mentioned in the newspapers do for you? All other things being equal, of any two lawyers, two doctors, or two executives, the one that gets mentioned in the newspaper has the career edge.

There are also numerous ways to leverage your published releases so that they work for you again and again. Similar to when I get an article published, I don't count on anyone in particular seeing my news release when it first appears. If those I am trying to influence do see it, I consider that a bonus. Once the release is published, I carefully clip it, paste it up, and make an attractive reprint on good bond paper.

I now have produced a document that I can add to my continuing portfolio of career marketing materials, which includes, by this time, a list of speaker's topics, perhaps a published article, and perhaps another person's article in which I am mentioned. All of these types of materials, plus biographies, fact sheets, photos, and other supporting background information, make up the components of what is called a press kit.

You don't need a big budget to produce a simple, personal, effective press kit. In fact, if you follow the suggestions in this book you will essentially be developing a press kit as you go along. As you will see in Chapter 21 (on getting on radio and TV), these materials come in handy in influencing program hosts to invite you as a guest on their shows.

OTHER PUBLICITY STRATEGIES

If you are willing to spend a little money, you might wish to have a logo and personalized stationery developed. This, of course, will depend on your overall career goals, the type of organization in which you are presently employed, and your personal finances. Designing an original, personalized logo can cost a minimum of $300, not including press and printing fees.

What is a logo? A logo is a pictorial representation of the image you want to create. It can be a picture or design with stylized letters. It should be uplifting and present you in a unified way. We have all lived with logos all our lives. The Texaco Star, the distinctive Coca-Cola script, and even the envelopes we get from the IRS are familiar examples of logos.

Another strategy in becoming your own press agent is to conduct surveys of interest to professionals in your industry. This need not be complicated. As an example, I lectured the National Capital Speakers Association on the topic of using articles to market your speaking capabilities. The night I was speaking there were 50 members and guests in attendance. As part of my presentation, I invited the group to share with me how I was going to generate an article right in front of their eyes.

I asked the group how many wanted to get published, and all 50 hands went up. Then I asked how many had ever been published, and approximately 38 hands went up. How many had used the article to market their speaking capabilities? Twenty-nine hands went up. How many were still using the article as a marketing too? Fourteen hands went up, and so on. In other words, in speaking to a group of Washington, D.C., area speakers, I was then able to produce a survey-type article entitled "Using Articles to Market Your Speaking Capabilities," which cited actual statistics based on this captive audience I was surveying.

I was similarly able to survey the area's management consultants. These types of surveys are always of great interest to the press. They can be submitted as articles or as news releases. If they are submitted as news releases, the first sentence might start out something like "Author Jeff Davidson recently surveyed 50 local management consultants on how they use articles to market their practice . . ."

Obviously, all of the above takes work. However, it all can be handled without disrupting your full-time job responsibilities. Figure 18–3 (on the next page) depicts a hypothetical week in the life of a career marketer.

The immense impact and importance of the media today is often misunderstood. One issue of *The New York Times* Sunday edition bombards us with more bits of information than an average person in 1888 was exposed to in his or her entire lifetime. Today there are over 10,000 publications listed in *Bacon's Publicity Checker, Working Press of the Nation,* and other similar directories covering every possible interest group. Some 99 percent of American households have one or more television sets, and radio has a good deal of impact also. There are ten times as many radio stations today as when television was first developed. Although you may have never considered it before, taking the time now to plan your media strategy and establishing good relationships with the media will prove invaluable in your future career marketing efforts.

Always be truthful and maintain integrity when dealing with the media. The relationship and reputation maintained with these keepers of public opinion will continue to gain in importance as your career star continues to rise.

Figure 18–3. Notes from the calendar of a strategic career marketer.

	SUNDAY	MONDAY	TUESDAY	WEDNESDAY	THURSDAY	FRIDAY	SATURDAY
AM	Read and clip newspaper articles and items of interest.		Discuss project plans with boss.		Listen to motivational cassette during commute.		
LUNCH		meet with peers for lunch.		meet with higher-up for lunch.		Review job & career marketing tasks for next week.	
PM	Note: Once a month update internal achievements list. volunteer for a community project, send action letters						
EVENING	to key individuals and meet with a mentor or career coach.	Scan professional journals. Add to clip file. Call colleagues network.	Speak to local group or work on an article. Attend seminar.	Stay late at work to help a colleague.		Stop off at company watering hole.	

Chapter 19 _____

Getting
Certified

*Every man is free to rise as far as he's able or
willing, but it's only the degree to which he thinks
that determines the degree to which he'll rise.*

Ayn Rand

We look to certification and licensing as a way of judging
the credentials and experience of a professional. It lets us know
that the professionals we hire have passed certain examinations
or qualifications set by their industry. Institutionalized license
procedures such as "MD" tell us that the person has completed
the training necessary to meet standards set by law. Dentists have
DDS after their names, indicating successful completion of training and an examination. A Certified Public Accountant (CPA) sig-
nifies a certification of quality in the profession of accounting.

You may be interested in certification as it concerns you. What
are some career advancement benefits of being certified? What

kinds of professions provide certification? Are there any directories that can be used to identify associations and societies that
offer certification programs in your field?

What Is Certification?

Certification is frequently confused with accreditation and/or
licensing.

Accreditation applies to programs rather than individuals, generally those of a school, college, institute, or university. It is
granted by an association to organizations that meet standards
determined through initial and periodic evaluations.

Licensing applies to individuals and is granted by a political
body to people who meet predetermined qualifications. It is required by law before certain professionals can engage in certain
occupations, such as doctor or dentist.

Certification also applies to individuals. It is voluntarily granted
by an association to people who meet predetermined qualifications. A study conducted several years ago showed that more
than 250 associations and societies had professional certification
programs in place.

Following is a sampling of certification programs:

Certificate for Welding Inspectors
Certificate in Data Processing
Certification and Qualification of Quality Control Inspectors
Certification for Occupational Therapy Assistants
Certified Association Executive
Certified Commercial Investment Member
Certified Electronics Technician
Certified Financial Planner
Certified Laboratory Assistant
Certified Military Club Manager
Certified Professional Social Worker
Certified Safety Professional

Certified Shorthand Reporter
Chartered Financial Analyst

In most industries, the certification process involves an examination, a written code of ethics that professionals must sign, and a description of the experience the professional must have to warrant certification. Many industries are currently reviewing the worth of recertification as a way of helping members to stay abreast of new developments in their fields.

If certification in any field is to signify abilities and experience adequately, the process is necessarily rigorous. After all, if it were easy to become certified, the certification would soon be worth very little to its recipients and their clients. Many professionals complain about certification procedures as "jumping through too many hoops," but they know the process of applying and earning acceptance is essential for a truly professional designation.

When I began my management consulting work in 1975, I had no idea that I would soon start working toward certification. After a year, however, things I'd been hearing led me to write to the Institute for Management Consultants to inquire about their Certified Management Consultant (CMC) designation. When I realized how rigorous the process would be, I was motivated to work that much harder for certification. The requirements included five years of experience as a management consultant and at least one as a project manager. The applicant had to submit five client write-ups, including describing a client engagement detail, three client references, and three associate references. In addition, there was an interview by a panel of three, an application fee, an initiation fee, and annual dues.

I found out that one-third of the Certified Management Consultants came from large national consulting firms like Booz, Allen, Hamilton; and Lawrence Leiter and Associates. Another third come from major management advisory services, such as Price Waterhouse; and Peat, Marwick, Mitchell & Co. Very few were from small, relatively unknown firms, as was my situation. Nevertheless, as soon as I had the required years of experience, I began the application process. It took me nine months to complete it and be granted certification, but in 1982, I was accepted. I felt I had earned my CMC designation, but I also knew that it was really still up to me to reap the greatest possible benefits from it.

Benefits of Certification

Certification programs have benefits for the individuals receiving certification, as well as for the associations that give the certifications (see Figure 19–1). For individuals, the benefits are discussed below.

Recognition.

When you are able to use a designated certification label with your name, people inside and outside your own company recognize that you have a certain degree of expertise in your field. Even though they may not know anything about the certification requirements or the certifying association, they almost automatically determine that you are a serious, noteworthy professional.

Top-level approval.

It often is difficult to get the attention of top management for the work we do. But certification provides a chance for junior-level professionals to get fairly quick approval from the top.

Networking.

Certification provides occasions to become involved with the certifying association—attend conferences, speak at meetings, or simply have a common ground for discussions with others who are also certified. Typically, this generates a professional network of colleagues who will be some of your best contacts for advice,

Figure 19–1. Professional certification.

Like accountants and architects, management consultants have a professional organization—the Institute of Management Consultants—that certifies individuals who voluntarily submit to its accreditation process and meet strict membership requirements.

To be a Certified Management Consultant, or CMC, a consultant must have a proven track record of superior client service and must demonstrate a high level of professional competence before a qualifying panel of his peers.

Ethically, a CMC pledges to place client interests first; to maintain objectivity and independence of position at all times; to safeguard client information; and to accept only those assignments that will result in real benefit to the client.

Institute certification is a valuable aid to management in the quest for competent consulting. It's the mark of a professional.

 INSTITUTE OF MANAGEMENT CONSULTANTS
19 West 44th, New York, NY 10036
212-921-2885

information, and especially active support when you decide to seek your next job.

Continued development.

Involvement with other certified professionals allows you to keep up with the latest developments in your field and establishes channels for an interchange of information that crosses organizational boundaries. This also has important implications for career development, as you become more and more aware of the various options for employment among individuals in your profession.

Keeping current.

Because you are exposed to top professionals in your field, you are encouraged to keep your knowledge and abilities current. You may also do this by attending seminars and conferences offered through the certifying associations or by reading the newsletters, magazines, and other publications the association may distribute.

Self-assessment.

The process of applying for certification can be a valuable self-assessment and development tool as you prepare for the certifying examination and/or review your achievements in writing for the application. Many certifications require periodic up-dating, which allows you continued opportunities for reassessing your professional strengths and weaknesses.

Assuming leadership.

Not everyone in your field will be certified. Your certification puts you in a natural leadership position in your profession, giving you valuable visibility among those in your own profession, as well as outside it.

All these benefits, of course, are only as valuable as you make them become. By all means, *use* your certification. Add your designated title to your stationery and business cards. Make sure it is included when anything is written about you. Volunteer to serve on committees and speak at meetings of your certifying association. Submit written items to their publications. Take a leadership role in organizing and conducting any local meetings of professionals in your field. Get involved and stay involved to let your certification really work for you.

Certification programs also prove beneficial to employers. The president of one management consulting firm only looks at résumés of people who have a CMC (Certified Management Consultant). "It's a quick way for me to know immediately who is worth talking to," he says.

Directories of Certification Programs

Two directories list thousands of professional, trade, and technical associations and societies that offer certification programs. You can find them in the reference section of your local library. They are:

Gale's Encyclopedia of Associations.
National Trade and Professional Associations of the United States (NTPA).

Locate the group in your field and request detailed information about any certification programs available. As a professional, you have every right to try for certification.

Chapter 20

Video Presentations and Your Future

I know the price of success—dedication, hard work, and an unremitting devotion to the things you want to see happen.

Frank Lloyd Wright

Whether it's a video résumé, a half-hour interview on a local cable television program, a taped presentation on company benefits to new employees, or a three-minute spot on *Good Morning America*, the chances that video skills will come in handy in your career marketing are steadily increasing.

My first introduction to video came several years ago when I took a community college course. At six-foot-three and 185 pounds, I had always feared that on video I might come across as just long and lanky. To my great surprise, I was actually satisfied with how I appeared, and this certainly served as a confidence booster.

Later, after I began speaking professionally, I had presentations video-taped as a marketing tool. I got other speaking engagements by letting meeting planners view previous presentations. The tape was also valuable for self-assessment purposes. Seeing yourself on video tape is seeing yourself in a brand-new way.

Let's take a look at today's video revolution and examine some ways to take best advantage of it.

VIDEO SKILLS

Bert Decker, founder and president of Decker Communications, notes that video training has many applications, but its most valuable use is in giving personal feedback to help individual performance. Today's professionals in all fields can benefit from polished video skills. The *Harvard Business Review* recently predicted that media presentation skills will be required of most managers and executives by 1990. Such skills may already be widely used within your organization, as in teleconferencing, or in video-taped product demonstrations, public information programs, and other creative applications outside the company. As we see expanded use of television and video to communicate in all aspects of business, the need for these skills will naturally intensify.

If well prepared, you can accept this new situation with confidence and will be able to deliver a powerful, "larger-than-life" presentation. However, Maggie Bedrosian says that without the necessary training and experience on video, most speakers surrender the challenge to "the other guy (or gal)."

Let's say that your industry calls for proposals to present information on a massive international teleconference. You realize that you could reach 30,000 people worldwide who are interested in your specialty or field of expertise. Are you ready to volunteer?

What if you have a new product line to introduce to your sales team across the country and around the world, or you have an orientation program to conduct monthly at scattered sites? In these instances, you want to make sure that everyone receives exactly the same complete, accurate information. Bedrosian says video lets you guarantee the uniformity of your presentations. You can also prepare intensively for one high-impact program, which can be used repeatedly.

Because it is recorded on a single occasion, companies can afford to use their most productive and dynamic presenters. Whether the session is conducted in Hackensack, New Jersey, or Budapest, Hungary, all participants receive the same basic information. Are you involved yet in producing custom-tailored data for your organization?

In a world of video dating services and video therapist selection, video résumés cannot be far behind. And they aren't! One company, InterVIEW, provides videotape services for executives wishing more personal impact than the printed form allows. Paul Beaudry, president of InterVIEW, rehearses the job candidate in a few basic camera skills and then tapes some responses to standard interview questions. These video résumés function as a powerful preliminary screening before possible meetings. Could you convince an unseen potential employer/client of your skills via video?

Preparing for the Camera

Getting ready for the camera is important because the audience responds to your message at many levels. Obviously, the audience can hear you speak, but, even more effective, they can see you.

"Our impact on our audience is conveyed not only in our choice of words," according to Bert Decker, "but in how we say them." When properly controlled, the body is an amazing tool for communications in itself. The art of mime is a strong example.

Perhaps the best way to evaluate overall physical communication is one "piece" at a time, beginning with the head. These tips will also be helpful for television appearances.

Your face.

Your most important "televehicle" is your face. Don't worry about being overly expressive, and don't worry that your nose, teeth, and eyes are off center. There are almost no symmetrical faces in the world. Picture Katherine Hepburn, Albert Einstein, Lee Iacocca, Geraldine Ferraro, Ronald Reagan—expressive faces, not symmetrical faces.

You may want to accept makeup if it is offered before facing the camera. Fran Campbell, a specialist in this area, reports that both men and women can enjoy these benefits from TV makeup:

- As the lights and camera tend to flatten your features, makeup enhances your natural features.
- Makeup helps you look healthy, vital, and alert, which encourages viewers to be more attentive.
- A light dusting of translucent powder reduces the glare and sweat caused by studio lights. This replaces that nervous-sweaty look with one of relaxed assurance.

If makeup is not offered, do it yourself. Women may use their regular makeup, but apply it one touch heavier. You don't need the drama of stage makeup—just a hint beyond everyday. Both men and women may want to carry baby powder or another translucent powder and a large brush for applying it. If you're under the lights for a long period, check your "shine" level on each break. You can freely apply many layers of translucent powder before it shows.

Your clothes.

Your attire should underline your message, not argue with it. What you choose to wear should reinforce what you choose to say. People react to what you wear and how you wear it as well as to what you say. Whether this is an artificial or hypocritical standard is not the issue. The issue is that people do respond to what they see, so judge accordingly. Appropriate clothes on video are those that support, or at least don't distract from, your message. Because of the way the camera functions, Maggie Bedrosian advises that it is best to *avoid*:

- Stark white, red, or black in large quantity, as these colors bloom, bleed, or "wash out" on camera.
- Large, bold, high contrast designs or prints, as they scream for attention, upstaging you and your ideas.
- Large metallic decorations or jewelry, as they reflect lights or create distracting noises.
- Narrow, repeating stripes, such as herringbone, as they wave and weave on camera.

However, it is good to *choose*:

- Subdued or neutral colors appropriate to your style and skin-tone.
- A comfortable fit sitting or standing.
- Fuller skirts for women for ease of walking and attractive drape when sitting.
- Simple, clean necklines that don't interfere with microphone placement.

Glasses.

Overall, it is better, if possible, to avoid wearing glasses on camera. You may, however, wish (or need) to wear them for two reasons. First, you may need them to see the person to whom you are speaking or to read. Second, people may be accustomed to seeing you in glasses, and they may not readily recognize you without them. If you do need glasses, select those with nonglare rims. You may ask the video technician if they have a nonglare spray. The director might ask you to tilt the glasses down a fraction to reduce the glare. This may feel clumsy to you, but it is much less distracting than glare.

Eye contact.

Bedrosian offers these few guidelines for eye contact with the camera.

1. The camera is an eavesdropper. Usually you will be looking at the reporter, the other panelists, or the questioner while the camera eavesdrops. You don't need to look into the camera, and, in fact, it's better if you don't because theoretically you are supposed to "ignore" the camera in such a situation. If an interview lasts more than five minutes, you may find yourself talking to your partner—who turns away for a word with the stage manager or to take a sip of water. If this happens, keep natural eye contact with the reporter, who isn't even there! Remember, that your real audience is the unseen viewers, not the people in the studio. Keep your poise for that real audience.

2. The camera is a listener. Use direct eye contact with the camera only when you are talking directly to the audience. You can blink, but always return to the camera, the "eyes" of your audience. This can be difficult because it is contrary to normal speaking patterns. In our society, the listener generally maintains eye contact while the speaker may look away, look down, or even close his or her eyes in thought. In direct eye contact for video,

those natural motions are distracting, so address the camera with your eyes.

3. The camera is "one of the gang." Sometimes the camera is in the studio audience or in the group of people you are addressing. In that case you have eye contact with the camera just as if it were another audience member. Don't focus on it, but don't avoid brief contact.

Gestures.

Studios sometimes tell guests to "sit on their hands." This overstates the point that television is an intimate medium. The camera picks up slight nuances of face and gesture and they convey powerful impact. Your TV appearance is not theater, there is no need for sweeping motions, pounding fists, and other dramatic gestures, which can, indeed, interfere with your message. Instead, try for natural gestures. Imagine a natural barrier six inches below your shoulders and try to keep your hands below that level unless you have a particularly strong reason for being dramatic. Reassure yourself that this small-scale and intimate quality of video makes it a potent medium for people of spirit and conviction who might never otherwise address large audiences.

INTERVIEW BASICS

One video or television opportunity with the greatest potential for marketing is the interview show. You could appear on or host a local cable program or be a guest on a broadcast talk show. Your segment may run from three minutes to an hour, but the main guidelines, according to Bedrosian, remain the same:

- Present yourself as clearly and cleanly as possible.
- Don't go on to "sell" your specific product, service, or company.

• Drawing from a keen sense of humor or a unique talent will further color your personality and bring life to an otherwise ordinary interview.

Relax

How you look on camera is not entirely up to you. Lighting, camera angles, the setting the director selects—all of these have great impact on how you appear in the final product. Rarely do you have control in these areas. If invited, you may want to see yourself on the monitor, request a certain placement of lights, or ask to be filmed in a setting reflecting your work. Ordinarily, however, trust the professionals and don't worry about technical details.

People who are confident in their ability to communicate can do so more easily. This is the overall goal of video training. Tomorrow's executive will have a wealth of video technology with fingertip control. Your success depends on preparation today.

Chapter 21

Getting on Radio and TV

To punish me for my contempt of authority, fate made me an authority myself.

Albert Einstein

To gain visibility quickly, radio and television are natural media for self-promotion. The people responsible for programming what goes out over the airwaves generally welcome the chance to consider new ideas and information. This is especially true for the talk shows that rely on interviewing people who can provide interesting discussions of timely topics.

Consider the statistics. There are approximately 10,000 radio stations, between ten and 30 in most cities in the United States. Each metropolitan area also has about three to five local television stations in addition to the national networks. Not all the programming is entertainment or news; there are more than 4,500 radio, television, and cable talk shows and approximately

12 to 18 regular talk shows in any given metropolitan area. These talk shows may be daily or weekly, and their hosts are constantly seeking people who have expertise and/or opinions in a wide variety of areas.

This means that, arithmetically, getting on radio and TV really isn't so difficult. But it helps to understand the business and carefully plan your approach.

The Town Crier

The talk show is the ultimate colloquium of today's "video-oriented, high-tech world," claims superhost Phil Donahue. "It's town crier and it's lamplighter." Each year, over a million and a half guests are scheduled to appear on programs broadcast throughout the United States and Canada. You don't need to be a celebrity or even known at all—approximately 90 percent of all radio and TV talk show guests are "common" people, virtually unknown to the listening or viewing audience before they speak. Although some people take great pains and preparation before appearing on a show and hire agents or publicists, many media consultants agree that, with some information and a little effort, you can do a good job without paying a small fortune for coaching. I recommend that you get two books on how to appear on radio or TV from your local library and read them before guesting. *How to Get Publicity* by William Parker (Times Books) and *The Persuasion Explosion* by Art Stevenson (Acropolis Books), as well as many others, are very helpful.

Breaking In

My own experience with getting on radio and TV is probably typical of the way it has happened or can happen for many professionals. My first experience came as a result of teaching an adult education course and began when a radio station host saw my course in the catalogue and called to ask me for an interview.

I did the interview, and not a lot happened as a result, *except* that I asked for a copy of the tape so I could review it and improve my oral presentations. I found it quite helpful to be able to hear myself, and I set about to identify ways in which I could say things differently the next time. Additionally, hearing the tape gave me new angles on the information I'd presented, and I was able to turn it into a magazine article.

As I wrote more articles and gained more expertise to share with listening audiences, I began to develop a list of radio talk show hosts whose programs might be appropriate for me. I also developed packages of materials, or mini press kits, to send to hosts, indicating my background and the subjects I could address on the air. I got on about two shows for every 15 packages I sent out.

After I had been on six or eight radio talk shows, a program assistant at CBS Television saw one of my articles on career marketing and asked me to be on "CBS Nightwatch." I appeared on four separate segments, including one on working with a difficult boss and another on strategies for career marketing. From those appearances, I received invitations to be on more shows and also obtained a video tape of my segments for my own review. When I began writing books, my radio and TV appearances accelerated.

Getting on radio and television has a way of spiraling—the more exposure you get, the more shows you are asked to be on. But only you can take the first steps of identifying the shows and topics and offering your services.

Benefits for You

No matter what business you are in, and whether you work for a company or are self-employed, you can immediately derive benefits from being on radio and TV. People who know you, through your work or outside your work, eventually will hear or see you, or at the very least, they will learn that you were on a show. This means that they are likely to grant you a greater amount of professional expertise than they did previously, and they are likely to give greater credit to your ideas and opinions. Your exposure and visibility broaden well beyond your current position.

You may get some feedback from people who hear you on radio or watch you on TV. When you get good feedback, it helps your self-confidence and reminds you about your strengths. When you get less favorable feedback, you begin to see yourself in the eyes of others and you get an opportunity to work on correcting problems.

By all means, always ask for a video or a voice tape following your appearances. Reviewing them will give you a chance at self-correction. Think about your voice. Was it too nasal? Too high-pitched? Did you sound authoritative enough? Then think about the content. Did you ramble? Were you vague rather than precise? Did you leave out any key points? Did you talk in terms that could be readily understood by the average listener or viewer?

A great benefit of being on talk shows is that a good host often brings out the best in you. You find yourself saying things in ways you haven't said them before, and this opens up more new ideas and insights. When reviewing a tape from a show on which I've appeared, I always gain new ways of looking at my areas of professional interest. Frequently, this leads to new ideas for articles or even books.

The Show and the Topic

With so many radio and TV talk shows in a given area, it may seem difficult to determine the ones that would be appropriate for you. First, start with the shows you know. Those that you watch and listen to are likely to be the ones with audiences that might want to hear from you. Then it's relatively easy to cancel out the ones that are unlikely—those that may specialize in areas outside your field or those that use only a host answering questions from telephone callers. That still leaves many programs that you may not know about.

Your newspaper program guide is a good place to start finding out about the many various shows. Additionally, your local Chamber of Commerce is likely to be able to provide you with a list of local stations and shows. And that list may also include the names of programming contacts you'll need to approach with your ideas for your appearances.

To get into talk shows in a big way, purchase the *Talk Show Guest Directory*, by Mitchell P. Davis, which sells for about $25. Nearly 2,000 copies of the directory are now in circulation, making it one of radio's most widely used sources of topics and guests for interviewing and call-in programs. Write to: Broadcast Interview Source, 2500 Wisconsin Avenue, NW, Suite 930, Washington, DC 20007. And Joe Shafian is a known specialist in media placement in the Washington D.C. area.

Also, the list of radio and television station directories presented below will provide you with the names and addresses of thousands of media leads. However, they are somewhat expensive, priced mainly from $60 to more than $200.

Radio and Television Station Directories

Broadcasting/Cable Casting Yearbook
Broadcasting Publications, Inc.
1735 De Sales Street, NW
Washington, DC 20036

(Every radio, TV, and cable outlet in the United States is listed; this is the bible of the broadcasting industry.)

Working Press of the Nation
National Research Bureau
310 South Michigan Avenue
Chicago, IL 60604

(A five-directory set of newspapers, magazines, TV and radio, feature writers, and internal publications. A very good overall media guide.)

Public Relations Plus
P.O. Box 329
Washington Depot, CT 06794

(Offers five focused directories: *New York Publicity Directory*, *Metro California Media*, *TV Publicity Outlets Nationwide*, *Cable TV Publicity Outlets*, and *The Family Page Directory*.)

National Radio Publicity Directory
Peter Glenn Publications
17 East 48th Street
New York, NY 10017

(A directory of talk shows with good topic indexing.)

Radio Programming Profile
BF Communications, Inc.
40 Railroad Avenue
Glen Head, NY 11545

(Three times a year, publishes large-market and small-market volumes of talk show contact information.)

Spot Radio Rates and Data
Standard Rate and Data Service
3004 Glenview Road
Wilmette, IL 60091

(12 issues; also highlights all the other media. There is little direct talk show information, but air time prices are shown.)

Larimi Radio Contacts
Larimi Communications Associates
151 East 50th Street
New York, NY 10022

(Provides names and addresses of 3,000 local, network, and syndicated radio shows featuring guest interviews. 1,100 pages in the annual edition with a monthly update.)

Hudson's Washington News Media Contacts
7315 Wisconsin Avenue
Bethesda, MD

(The full service directory of Washington contacts and national contacts in Washington, D.C.)

United Way Media Factbook
Communications Office of the United Way of the National Capitol Area
95 M Street, SW
Room 306
Washington, DC 20024

(200 plus pages give information about local publications and media; published July 1985. A true bargain.)

East Coast Publicity Directory
IMS/Ayer
426 Pennsylvania Avenue
Fort Washington, PA 19034

(Massachusetts to Florida, everything in print and media.)

Weiner's Directory of Public Relations Services
Public Relations Publishing Co., Inc.
888 Seventh Avenue
New York, NY 10106

(No PR firms are listed, just subcontractors.)

Cable Services Report
Local Programming National Cable Association
1724 Massachusetts Avenue, NW
Washington, DC 20036

(Provides names and addresses of more than 800 cable television systems throughout the United States.)

Once you have a rather complete list of shows, watch and listen to as many as possible. If there is some doubt as to whether a show is appropriate for you, assume it is until you know otherwise. That is, approach producers or hosts at that show with your ideas and materials, and let them decide.

Determining the topics that you might want to discuss on a radio or TV show may seem a bit difficult at first, but it does get easier as you become more familiar with what is wanted and with what you have to offer. Obviously, you first need to examine your own areas of experience, expertise, and special knowledge. You may need to think about an "angle"—some aspects of your knowledge or expertise that would make it all the more interesting to a listening or viewing audience. Below are some ideas:

- New angle—does your expertise lend itself to in-depth discussion of something currently in the news?
- Trend angle—could your expertise enable you to shed light on a current trend or identify a new one?
- Local angle—does your expertise put you in the position of being a "local" spokesperson on a topic of national significance?
- Controversy angle—has your expertise led you to opinions that are on one side or the other of a stimulating public debate?

In other words, selection of topics is a time to get creative—to develop as many ideas as possible for areas that you can discuss with a certain amount of authority. When you put your mind to it, you'll find you have more to say than you think. For example, maybe you had to research the impact of a new municipal tax on your company. Now you're in a position to discuss its general impact on the air. Or, maybe your work in the area of financial management has given you some good ideas for tips on how people can streamline their personal financial management. Offer to share these on radio and TV.

Public Access Television

A good outlet for starting to get exposure, practicing your approach, and testing your ideas is public access television. If your community has cable TV, it probably has public access channels that create free air time for amateurs. Cable operators provide these to fill up otherwise blank channels and to allow groups and individuals to air their messages. They allow you to develop your own program, using one or more video cameras at the public access studios. Since the resources aren't large and your production expertise is probably limited, you'll want to keep anything you produce for public access as simple as possible, perhaps just you being interviewed by one other person.

To get on public access television, you must find the administering body. Often this is the cable company in your area, or it may be a municipal agency. You'll need to work closely with the administering body to develop your program and schedule your air time. If you find that your ideas for a program fit within their guidelines, it is well worth the effort. You get experience and a good deal of knowledge about production and programming.

Using Your Press Kit

Once you target shows and develop some likely topics, you'll need to assemble the items we've discussed throughout this book into a press kit to send to the show producers and/or hosts. This is a package of written material (preferably presented in an attractive folder) that tells media sources what you *have done* and what you *can do* on a show (see also Chapter 18).

Items that can be used in your press kit include:

- Biographical documents (a biography or other chronology of your experience as it pertains to what you would present on radio and TV).
- Clips (samples of any pertinent material you have authored).
- Articles in which you are mentioned (obviously authored by someone else).
- Press releases (news about you).
- Media contact sheet (list of previous media contacts, including print media).
- Position paper (a statement by you that indicates your viewpoints on the topic you would discuss).
- Letters of endorsement.
- Photographs (for television press kits).
- Fact sheets, brochures.

When you send your press kit, include a personalized cover letter for each station, which briefly summarizes why you should be considered for a talk show, what show you have in mind, and where you can be reached for scheduling.

If you are in a very large metropolitan area with many radio and television stations and shows, you may want to consider having your material sent out by a media mailing service. The same is true if you get to the point where you feel you need regional or national coverage. Such services can develop a list for your materials and mail them out for you. Many will also do the duplicating and collating work for your press kit.

If you are sending out your own press kit materials, do not just send them to the stations with a "Dear Sirs" letter. Phone the station and find out exactly who is responsible for making decisions concerning the show you have in mind. It may be the show's host, or it may be the producer or a programming director. Send your kit and address your cover letter directly to that individual. Your materials are much more likely to get attention that way, and the individual involved is more likely to feel you merit some kind of response.

Make follow-up phone calls within three days after the mailing, and be prepared to summarize your ideas in a few words for those who might not have read your press kit. Also, think of any additional information you might add at this point—"plugs" that could make your ideas seem all the more interesting. Sometimes, it is best to call first, generating interest, then mail, then call again.

Organize a file concerning your mailings—names and addresses of individual recipients, copies of cover letters, and notes about response. Review this file from time to time and let it be a "tickler" to remind you when you have not had a response after several weeks.

Homework, Then Interviews

When you are asked to be on television or radio, watch or listen to that particular show ahead of time as much as possible to familiarize yourself with the format and the personality of the host. This will give you an idea of the types of questions asked and whether you'll be doing a "monologue" type discussion or simply giving brief answers. If possible, contact the host ahead of time to find out exactly what he or she intends to ask and what areas of your topic are to be emphasized.

Develop your own list of likely questions and answers, and rehearse them ahead of time. Additionally, think of the key points you want to make. How will you make them if you aren't asked a question about them directly? A good way to do that is simply to insert into the conversation a statement that begins with, "I am often asked . . ." Then, you can go on to answer your own questions.

Another part of preparation is to think about the "personality" you want to project. Do you want to come across as authoritative, forceful, intellectual, humorous, or what? When you see others who come across this way, what do they say and do that helps that to happen? It helps to identify radio and television role models whose styles you can emulate and adapt to your own. The tips and suggestions in Chapter 20 on using video tape are certainly useful in preparation for your radio or TV appearance.

Once you have determined your style and developed a list of questions and answers, rehearse on audio tape, on video, or just in front of your mirror. You'll be amazed how much self-correction you'll want to do before you go on the air. The mere fact of knowing you are well rehearsed will help you to be relaxed and self-confident when you appear.

After the Show

After the show, as already noted, ask for a tape. It will help you immensely in future radio and television appearances. If things went well, ask for a letter thanking you. You might feel a little hesitant asking for such a letter, but if you can include a letter or two from ABC or CNN in your press kit, your next talk show visit may follow quickly. Also, keep in touch with the people at the show where you appeared. Send *them* a letter after your appearance and contact them later with ideas for future appearances.

There is a mystique about radio and television that makes many people think it applies only to "performers"—those individuals who have an ability to entertain and interest the audience. But if you start watching and listening to many talk shows, you will soon realize that most of the people being interviewed have no performance background at all. Instead, they have figured out how to "package" themselves and their messages in an informative way. And this is something that, with a little effort and patience, *you* can do.

Leveraging Media Appearances

By now you know how the strategic career marketer leverages exposure so that it can be used again and again. Following your media appearance on radio or TV, I recommend duplicating your audio or video tape, if you are pleased with it, so that you can send it out to others, thereby increasing your chances of being invited to be a guest. Also, as previously mentioned, review the tapes carefully and see if you surprise yourself with any new thoughts, ideas, or twists on the work that you do or the services you provide. Have the tape transcribed and then carefully review it to see if you can quickly fashion an article or perhaps two out of the transcription. Log in the date, time, and topic of this most recent media appearance on your media contact sheet so that your personal press kit always remains up-to-date. Finally, reflect on your career marketing goals, and how your most recent media appearance accelerated the rate at which you can meet those goals.

Professional exposure is your ticket to the world. Before reading this book, if you hadn't taken step one toward strategically marketing your career, all this may seem a bit overwhelming. However, once you get started, or if you have already started, you quickly experience how small career marketing victories add up and help you to board an upward spiral that never need stop.

Perhaps the best definition of success—certainly career success—that I have come across is from South Carolina consultant and speaker Al Walker, who defines it as "making the most of the best that is within you every day by having a goal, being committed to it, and underscoring it with enthusiasm."

The work that you do, and the service that you provide, can make a difference. Strategic career marketing will help to expose others to the good you are already doing.

Appendix A
Professional Trade Associations

COMMUNICATIONS, GRAPHICS, PRINTING

American Association of Advertising Agencies
666 Third Avenue
New York, NY 10017
(212) 682-2500

Direct Marketing Association
6 East 43rd Street
New York, NY 10017
(212) 689-4977

Graphic Communications International
1900 L Street, NW
Washington, DC 20036
(202) 462-1400

International Association of Business Communicators
870 Market Street, #940
San Francisco, CA 94102
(415) 433-3400

Printing Industries of America
1730 North Lynn Street
Arlington, VA 22209
(703) 841-8100

Public Relations Society of America
845 Third Avenue
New York, NY 10022
(212) 826-1750

COMPUTERS, ADP

American Electronics Association
2670 Hanover
P.O. Box 10045
Palo Alto, CA 94303
(415) 857-9300

Association of Information System Professionals
1015 North York Road
Willow Grove, PA 19090
(215) 657-6300

Association for Systems Management
24587 Bagley Road
Cleveland, OH 44138
(216) 243-6900

Data Entry Management Association
Box 16711
Stamford, CT 06905
(203) 967-3500

Data Processing Management Association
505 Busse Highway
Park Ridge, IL 60068
(312) 693-5070

Information Industry Association
555 New Jersey Avenue, NW
Washington, DC 20001
(202) 544-1969

Office Automation Society International
15269 Mimosa, Suite B
Dumfries, VA 22026
(703) 690-3880

Society for Information Management
Suite 600
111 East Wacker Drive
Chicago, IL 60601
(312) 644-6610

Special Interest Group on Business Data Processing and Management
c/o Association for Computing Machinery
11 West 42nd Street
New York, NY 10036
(212) 869-7440

CONSTRUCTION, CONTRACTING

Associated Builders & Contractors, Inc.
729 15th Street, NW
Washington, DC 20005
(202) 637-8800

Associated General Contractors of America
1957 E Street, NW
Washington, DC 20006
(202) 393-2040

National Association of Home Builders
15th and M Streets, NW
Washington, DC 20005
(202) 822-0200

National Association of the Remodeling Industry
1901 North Moore Street, #805
Arlington, VA 22209
(703) 276-7600

American Society of Appraisers
11800 Sunrise Valley Drive
Suite 400
Reston, VA 22091
(703) 620-3838

American Society of Professional Estimators
6911 Richmond Highway, #230
Alexandria, VA 22091
(703) 765-2700

Building Owners and Managers Association International
1250 Eye Street, NW
Washington, DC 20005
(202) 289-7000

Financial Executives Institute
10 Madison Avenue
P.O. Box 1938
Morristown, NJ 07860
(201) 898-4600

Independent Insurance Agents of America, Inc.
100 Church Street
New York, NY 10007
(212) 285-4250

National Association of Bank Women
500 North Michigan Avenue
Suite 1400
Chicago, IL 60611
(312) 661-1700

National Association of Professional Insurance Agents
400 North Washington Street
Alexandria, VA 22314
(703) 836-9340

National Association of Realtors
430 North Michigan Avenue
Chicago, IL 60611
(312) 329-8200

National Security Traders Association
One World Trade Center, #4511
New York, NY 10048
(212) 524-0484

Securities Industry Association
120 Broadway, 35th Floor
New York, NY 10271
(212) 608-1500

FEDERAL AND STATE EMPLOYEES

American Federation of Government Employees
80 F Street, NW
Washington, DC 20001
(202) 737-8700

American Federation of State, County, and Municipal Employees
1625 L Street, NW
Washington, DC 20036
(202) 452-4800

American Public Works Association
1313 East 60th Street
Chicago, IL 60637
(312) 667-2200

American Society for Public Administration
1120 G Street, NW
Suite 500
Washington, DC 20005
(202) 393-7878

Assembly of Governmental Employees
655 15th Street, NW
Suite 300
Washington, DC 20005
(202) 371-1123

Federal Law Enforcement Officers Association
106 Cedarhurst Avenue
Selden, NY 11784
(516) 698-0179

Federal Managers Association
2300 South 9th Street
Suite 104
Arlington, VA 22204
(703) 892-4418

National Federation of Federal Employees
2020 K Street, #200
Washington, DC 20006
(202) 862-4400

FINANCE

American Bankers Association
1120 Connecticut Avenue, NW
Washington, DC 20036
(202) 467-4000

Million Dollar Round Table
2340 River Road
Des Plaines, IL 60018
(312) 298-1120

American Institute of Real Estate
  Appraisers
430 North Michigan Avenue
Chicago, IL 60611
(312) 329-8559

Mortgage Banker Association of
  America
1125 15th Street, NW
Washington, DC 20005
(202) 861-6500

HEALTH, ALLIED HEALTH

American Academy of Family
  Physicians
1740 West 92nd Street
Kansas City, MO 64114
(816) 333-9700

Group Health Association of
  America
624 9th Street, NW
Washington, DC 20001
(202) 737-4311

American Health Care Association
1200 15th Street, NW
8th Floor
Washington, DC 20005
(202) 833-2050

Health Physics Society
1340 Old Chain Bridge Road
Suite 300
McLean, VA 22101
(703) 790-1745

Association for Research, Administration, Professional Coun-
  cils and Societies
1900 Association Drive
Reston, VA 22091
(703) 476-3430

Healthcare Financial Management
  Association
Suite 500
1900 Spring Road
Oak Brook, IL 60521
(800) 252-4362

Medical Group Management Association
Suite 900
1355 S. Colorado Blvd.
Denver, CO 80222
(303) 753-1111

National Health Lawyers Association
Suite 120
522 21st Street, NW
Washington, DC
(202) 833-1100

LEISURE, TOURISM, TRAVEL

American Association for Leisure and Recreation
1900 Association Drive
Reston, VA 22091
(703) 476-3400

Travel and Tourism Research Association
Box 8066 Foothill Station
Salt Lake City, UT 84108
(801) 581-3351

American Hotel and Motel Association
888 Seventh Avenue
New York, NY 10019
(212) 265-4506

National Recreation and Park Association
3101 Park Center Drive
Alexandria, VA 22302
(703) 820-4940

American Society of Travel Agents
MacArthur Boulevard
Washington, DC 20007
(202) 965-7520

Travel Industry 4400 Association of America
1899 L Street, NW
Suite 600
Washington, DC 20036
(202) 293-1433

MANUFACTURING

Equipment and Tool Institute
1545 Waukengan Road
Glenview, IL 60025
(312) 729-8550

Apparel Manufacturers Association, Inc.
1440 Broadway
New York, NY 10018
(212) 398-0770

Chemical Manufacturers Association
2501 M Street, NW
Washington, DC 20037
(202) 887-1100

Industrial Fabrics Association International
345 Cedar Building
St. Paul, MN 55101
(612) 222-2508

National Association of Manufacturers
1776 F Street, NW
Washington, DC 20006
(202) 637-3000

National Office Products Association
301 N. Fairfax Street
Alexandria, VA 22314
(703) 549-9040

PROFESSIONAL SERVICES

American Bar Association
750 North Lake Shore Drive
Chicago, IL 60611
(312) 998-5000

American Institute of Certified Public Accountants
1211 Avenue of the Americas
New York, NY 10036
(212) 575-6200

American Institute of Architects
1735 New York Avenue, NW
Washington, DC 20006
(202) 626-7300

American Society of Women Public Accountants
35 East Wacker Drive
Chicago, IL 60601
(312) 726-9030

Association of Management Consultants
500 North Michigan Avenue
Chicago, IL 60611
(312) 226-1261

Institute of Management Consultants
19 West 44th Street
New York, NY 10036
(212) 921-2885

National Association of Accountants
919 Third Avenue
New York, NY 10022
(212) 754-9700

National Society of Accountants
1010 North Fairfax Street
Alexandria, VA 22314
(703) 549-6400

RETAILING

American Booksellers Association
122 East 42nd Street
New York, NY 10168
(212) 867-9060

American Retail Federation
1616 H Street, NW
Washington, DC 20006
(202) 783-7971

Food Marketing Institute
1750 K Street, Suite 700
Washington, DC 20006
(202) 452-8444

National Home Furnishing Association
405 Merchandise Mart Plaza
Chicago, IL 60654
(312) 836-0777

National Restaurant Association
311 First Street
Washington, DC 20001
(202) 638-6100

National Retail Merchants Association
100 West 31st Street
New York, NY 10001
(212) 244-8780

SMALL BUSINESSES

American Business Women's Association
P.O. Box 8728
9100 Ward Parkway
Kansas City, MO 64114
(816) 361-6621

American Chamber of Commerce Executives
1133 15th Street, NW, Suite 620
Washington, DC 20005
(202) 296-1762

American Federation of Small Business
407 South Dearborn Street
Chicago, IL 60605
(312) 427-0206

Center for Small Business
U.S. Chamber of Commerce
1615 H Street, NW
Washington, DC 20062
(202) 463-5503

National Federation of Independent Business
150 West 20th Avenue
San Mateo, CA 94403
(415) 341-7441

National Small Business United
1604 K Street, NW
Washington, DC 20006
(202) 296-7400

SUPERVISION, ADMINISTRATION, MANAGEMENT

American Management Association
135 West 50th Street
New York, NY 10020
(212) 586-8100

American Society for Public
Administration
1120 G Street, NW
Suite 500
Washington, DC 20005
(202) 393-7878

American Society of Association
Executives
1575 Eye Street, NW
Washington, DC 20005
(202) 626-2723

Data Processing Management Association
505 Busse Highway
Park Ridge, IL 60068
(312) 693-5070

Employment Management Association (EMA)
1100 Raleigh Building
Raleigh, NC 27601
(919) 821-1435

Human Resource Planning Society
(HRPS)
P.O. Box 2553
Grand Central Station
New York, NY 10163
(212) 837-0630

International Personnel Management Association (IPMA)
1617 Duke Street
Alexandria, Va 22314
(703) 549-7100

National Association of Personnel
Consultants (NAPC)
1432 Duke Street
Alexandria, VA 22314

National Management Association
2210 Arbor Boulevard
Dayton, OH 45439
(513) 294-0421

WHOLESALERS

Durable Goods

Automotive Warehouse Distributors Association
9140 Ward Parkway, Suite 200
Kansas City, MO 64114
(816) 444-3500

National Association of Wholesaler-Distributors
1725 K Street, NW
Washington, DC 20006
(202) 872-0885

National Building Material Distributors
1701 Lake Avenue
Suite 170
Glenview, IL 60025
(312) 724-6900

Non-durable Goods

National Wine Distributors Association
102 East Ontario Street, Suite 760
Chicago, IL 60611
(312) 951-8878

United Fresh Fruit & Vegetable Association
North Washington and Madison Streets
Alexandria, VA 22314
(703) 836-3410

Appendix B
Magazines and Journals

Administrative Management
AMS
2360 Maryland Road
Willow Grove, PA 19090
(215) 659-4300

Association Management
Magazine of the American Society
   of Association Executives
1575 Eye Street
Washington, DC 20005
(202) 626-2708

Bureaucrat
Bureaucrat, Inc.
P.O. Box 347
Arlington, VA 22210
(202) 287-6070

Business
Georgia State University
College of Business Administra-
   tion
Atlanta, GA 30303
(404) 658-4253

Business and Society Review
Warren, Gorham & Lamont, Inc.
210 South Street
Boston, MA 02111
(617) 423-2020

Business Marketing
Crain Communications, Inc.
220 E. 42nd Street
New York, NY 10017
(212) 210-0100

Business Quarterly
University of Western Ontario
1393 Western Road
London, Ontario, N6A 5B9 Canada
(519) 679-3222

Business Week
McGraw-Hill, Inc.
1221 Avenue of the Americas
New York, NY 10020
(212) 997-3896

California Management Review
University of California
Graduate School of Business Administration
350 Barrows Hall
Berkeley, CA 94720
(415) 642-7159

Canadian Manager
Canadian Institute of Management
2175 Sheppard Avenue East
Suite 110
Willowdale, Ontario M2J 1W8 Canada
(416) 493-0155

Chief Executive (U.S.)
645 Fifth Avenue
New York, NY 10022
(212) 826-2100

Contract Management
6728 Old McLean Village Drive
McLean, VA 22101
(703) 442-0137

Credit & Financial Management
National Association of Credit Management
475 Park Avenue South
New York, NY 10016
(212) 578-4410

Engineering Economist
Engineering Economist AITE
25 Technology Park/Atlanta
Norcross, GA 30092
(404) 449-0460

Executive (Canada)
c/o Airmedia
2973 Weston Road
Weston, Ontario M9M2T2, Canada
(416) 741-1112

Financial Executive
Financial Executives Institute
10 Madison Avenue
P.O. Box 1938
Morristown, NJ 07960
(201) 898-4600

Forbes
Forbes, Inc.
60 Fifth Avenue
New York, NY 10011
(212) 620-2200

Fortune
Time, Inc.
541 N. Fairbanks Court
Chicago, IL 60611
(312) 329-6800 or (800) 972-8302

Futurist
World Future Society
4916 Saint Elmo Avenue
Bethesda, MD 20814
(301) 656-8274

Harvard Business Review
Harvard University
Editorial Department
Soldiers' Field, Teele Hall
Boston, MA 02163
(800) 225-5355

Human Resource Management
University of Michigan
Division of Management Education
Graduate School of Business Administration
Ann Arbor, MI 48104
(313) 763-0212

Human Resource Planning
Human Resource Planning Society
Grand Central Station
P.O. Box 2553
New York, NY 10017
(212) 490-6387

In Business
J.G. Press, Inc.
Box 323, 18 South 7th Street
Emmaus, PA 18047
(215) 967-4135

Inc.
38 Commercial Wharf
Boston, MA 02110
(617) 227-4700

Industrial Distribution
Technical Publishing
875 Third Avenue
New York, NY 10022
(212) 605-9400

Industrial Management
Institute of Industrial Engineers, Inc.
25 Technology Park/Atlanta
Norcross, GA 30092
(404) 449-0460

Industrial Management
McGraw-Hill, Inc.
1221 Avenue of the Americas
New York, NY 10020
(212) 997-1221

Journal of Accountancy
American Institute of Certified Public Accountants
1211 Avenue of the Americas
New York, NY 10036-8775
(212) 575-6200

Journal of Marketing
American Marketing Association
250 South Wacker Drive
Chicago, IL 60606
(312) 648-0536

Journal of Personal Selling and Sales Management
145 North Avenue, Suite G
Hartland, WI 53029
(800) 421-5394

Journal of Property Management
National Association of Realtors
430 North Michigan Avenue
Chicago, IL 60611
(312) 661-1930

Journal of Retailing
New York University
Institute of Retail Management
202 Tisch Hall, Washington
   Square
New York, NY 10003
(212) 598-2285

Journal of Small Business Manage-
   ment
West Virginia University Bureau
   of Business Research
P.O. Box 6025
Morgantown, WV 26506
(304) 293-0111

Manage
National Management Association
2210 Arbor Boulevard
Dayton, OH 45439
(513) 294-0421

Management
Superintendent of Documents
Government Printing Office
Washington, DC 20402
(202) 783-3238

Management Accounting
10 Paragon Drive
P.O. Box 433
Montvale, NJ 07645
(201) 573-9000

Magazine of Bank Administration
Bank Administration Institute
60 Gould Center
2550 Golf Road
Rolling Meadows, IL 60008
(312) 228-6200

Management Review
American Management Association
135 West 50th Street
New York, NY 10020
(212) 586-8100

Management Today
30 Lancaster Gate
London, W2 3LP England
(01) 402-4200

Management World
AMS
2360 Maryland Road
Willow Grove, PA 19090
(215) 659-4300

Managerial Planning
Planning Executive Institute
Box 70
Oxford, OH 45056
(513) 523-4185

Managers Magazine
LIMRA
P.O. Box 208
Hartford, CT 06141
(203) 677-0033

Marketing Communications
475 Park Avenue South
New York, NY
(212) 725-2300

Marketing News
250 South Wacker Drive
Chicago, IL 60606
(312) 648-0536

New Management
Graduate School of Business
    Administration
University of Southern California
Los Angeles, CA 90089
(213) 743-5304

Office Administration and Auto-
    mation
Geyer-McAllister Publications
51 Madison Avenue
New York, NY 10010
(212) 689-4411

Personnel
American Management Associa-
    tion
135 West 50th Street
New York, NY 10020
(212) 903-8067

Personnel Administrator
American Society for Personnel
    Administration
606 North Washington Street
Alexandria, VA 22314
(703) 548-3440

Personnel Journal
245 Fisher Avenue B-2
Costa Mesa, CA 92627
(714) 751-1883

Personnel Management
Personnel Publications, Ltd.
1 Hills Place
London, W1R 1AG ENGLAND
(01) 734-1773

Practicing Manager
Australian Administrative Staff
    College
Kunyung Road
Mt. Eliza, Victoria 3930
Australia
(03) 787-4211

Program Manager
Defense Systems Management
    College
Department of Research and In-
    formation
Fort Belvoir, VA 22060
(703) 664-5082

Public Personnel Management
1617 Duke Street
Alexandria, VA 22314
(703) 549-7100

Public Relations Journal
Public Relations Society of Amer-
    ica
845 Third Avenue
New York, NY 10022
(212) 826-1750

Public Relations Quarterly
P.O. Box 311
Rhineback, NY 12572
(914) 876-2081

Public Relations Review
7100 Baltimore Blvd.,
Suite 500
College Park, MD 20740
(301) 927-3998

Sales and Marketing Management
633 Third Avenue
New York, NY 10017
(212) 986-4800

Sloan Management Review
Massachusetts Institute of Technology
50 Memorial Drive
Cambridge, MA 02139
(617) 253-7150

Supervision
National Research Bureau
424 North 3rd Street
Burlington, IA 52601
(319) 752-5415

Supervisory Management
American Management Association
135 West 50th Street
New York, NY 10020
(212) 586-8100

Training
Lakewood Publications, Inc.
731 Hennepin Avenue
Minneapolis, MN 55403
(612) 333-0417

Training and Development Journal
1630 Duke Street
Box 1443
Alexandria, VA 22313
(703) 683-8100

Venture
521 5th Avenue
New York, NY 10175-0028
(212) 682-7373

Appendix C
Newsletters

There are over 8,000 newsletters in the United States today, and the number is steadily growing. The *Oxbridge Directory of Newsletters* or the *Newsletter Yearbook Directory* are particularly useful sources of information about the variety of available newsletters. Following is a brief listing of management and career-type newsletters.

Creative Management
Business Research Publications
817 Broadway
New York, NY 10003

The Effective Manager
Warren, Gorham & Lamont Inc.
210 South Street
Boston, MA 02111

Effective Executive
The Dartnell Corporation
4660 Ravenswood Avenue
Chicago, IL 60640

Foremanship
The Dartnell Corporation
4660 Ravenswood Avenue
Chicago, IL 60640

Productivity
P.O. Box 3456
Stamford, CT

Productivity and Performance
Office Edition
Bureau of Business Practice, Inc.
24 Rope Ferry Road
Waterford, CT 06386

Successful Supervisor
The Dartnell Corporation
4660 Ravenswood Avenue
Chicago, IL 60640

Supervision for Technology & Elec-
tronics Management
Bureau of Business Practice, Inc.
24 Rope Ferry Road
Waterford, CT 06386

Appendix D
Media Directories

PRINT

Magazine Industry Marketplace
R. R. Bowker Company
245 West 17th Street
New York, NY 10011

The grandfather of the industry containing names and addresses of more than 5,000 periodicals.

Editor and Publisher Annual Directory of Syndicated Services
Editor and Publisher Company
575 Lexington Avenue
New York, NY 10011

Single issue per year provides a listing of syndicates supplying U.S. and foreign newspapers with news features and columns.

Media Guild International: Newspapers and News Magazines
Directories International, Inc.
150 5th Avenue
New York, NY 10011

Provides names and addresses of thousands of newspapers and news magazines both in the U.S. and abroad.

The Syndicated Columnist's Directory
Public Relations Publishing Company
888 7th Avenue
New York, NY 10106

Provides names and addresses of more than 800 syndicated newspaper columnists arranged by topic area or field.

BUSINESS PUBLICATIONS

Media Guide International: Business/Professional Publications
Directories International, Inc.
150 5th Avenue
New York, NY 10011

Provides names and addresses of more than 7,000 business and professional publications throughout the U.S. and internationally.

Internal Publications Directory
National Research Bureau Inc.
104 South Michigan Avenue
Chicago, IL 60603

Provides names and addresses of internal and external house organs published by North American companies and organizations, federal agencies, associations, and other professional groups.

Appendix E
For Further Reading

Andersen, Martin P., E. Ray Nichols, and Herbert W. Booth, *The Speaker and His Audience*. New York: Harper & Row, 1974.

Angel, Juvenal L., *The Complete Résumé Book & Job-Getter's Guide*. New York: Pocket Books, 1985.

Austin, Margaret F., *Bridges to Success: Finding Jobs and Changing Careers*. New York: John Wiley & Sons, 1983.

Barton, Paul E.,*Worklife Transitions: The Adult Learning Connection*. New York: McGraw-Hill, 1982.

Bastress, Frances, *The Relocating Spouses' Guide to Employment: Options and Strategies in the U.S. and Abroad*. Chevy Chase, MD: Woodley Publications, 1986.

Bedrosian, Margaret, *Speak Like a Pro*. New York: John Wiley & Sons, 1986.

Bliss, Edwin C., *Getting Things Done: The ABCs of Time Management*. New York: Charles Scribner Sons, 1976.

Bly, Robert W., and Gary Blake, *Dream Jobs: A Guide to Tomorrow's Top Careers*. New York: John Wiley & Sons, 1983.

Boll, Carl, *Executives Jobs Unlimited*. New York: Macmillan, 1980.

Bolles, Richard N., *What Color Is Your Parachute? A Practical Manual for Job-Hunters & Career Changers*. Berkeley: Ten Speed Press, 1981.

Bolles, Richard N., *The Three Boxes of Life*. Berkeley: Ten Speed Press, 1978.

Bostwick, Burdett, *Finding the Job You Have Always Wanted*. New York: John Wiley & Sons, 1977.

Boulgarides, James D., *Are You in the Right Job?* Englewood Cliffs, NJ: Monarch Press, 1984.

Bright, Deborah, *Gearing Up for the Fast Lane: The Challenging of Exceptional Performance*. New York: Random House, 1986.

Brown, Ronald Michael, *Practical Speechmaking*. Dubuque: W.C. Brown, 1970.

Burns, David, *Feeling Good: The New Mood Therapy*. New York: William Morrow, 1980.

Cohen, Herb, *You Can Negotiate Anything*. Chicago: Lyle Stuart, 1981.

Cohen, William A., *The Executives' Guide to Finding a Superior Job*. Saranac Lake, NY: AMACOM Books, 1980.

Cohen, William A., *How to Make It Big as a Consultant*. New York: AMACOM Books, 1985.

Connelly, J. Campbell, *A Manager's Guide to Speaking and Listening*. New York: AMACOM Books, 1967.

Connor, Richard A., Jr., and Jeffrey P. Davidson, *Marketing Your Consulting and Professional Services*. New York: John Wiley & Sons, 1985.

Davidson, Jeffrey P., *Marketing to the Fortune 500*. Homewood, IL: Dow Jones-Irwin, 1987.

Dickhut, Harold W., and Marvel J. Davis, *Professional Resume/Job Search Guide*. Chicago: Management Counselors, Inc., 1981.

Dubrin, Andrew J., *Winning at Office Politics*. New York: Ballantine Books, 1978.

Elsea, Dr. Janet, *First Impression, Best Impression*. New York: Simon & Schuster, 1986.

Engle, Peter H., *The Overachievers*. New York: Dial Press, 1976.

Feingold, Dr. S. Norman, and Norma Reno Miller. *Emerging Careers: New Occupations for the Year 2000 and Beyond*. Garrett Park: Garrett Park Press, 1983.

Feingold, Dr. S. Norman, and Avis Nicholson, *Getting Ahead: A Women's Guide to Career Success*. Washington, DC: Acropolis Books, 1983.

Feingold, Dr. S. Norman, and Dr. Leonard Perlman, *Making It on Your Own*. Washington, DC: Acropolis Books, 1985.

Figler, Howard, *The Complete Job-Search Handbook*. New York: Holt, Rinehart & Winston, 1980.

German, Donald R., and Joan W. German, *How to Find a Job When Jobs Are Hard to Find*. New York: AMACOM Executive Books, 1981.

Germann, Richard, and Diane Blumenson, *Working & Liking It*. New York: Fawcett Columbine Books, 1984.

Goldberg, Joan Rachel, *High Tech Career Strategies for Women*. New York: Macmillan, 1984.

Harragan, Betty Lehan, *Games Mother Never Taught You (Corporate Gamesmanship for Women)*. New York: Warner Books, 1977.

Hart, Lois Borland, *Moving Up!* Saranac Lake, NY: AMACOM Books, 1980.

Hensley, Dennis E., *Become Famous, Then Rich*. Indianapolis: R & R Newkirk, 1983.

Higginson, Margaret V., and Thomas L. Quick, *The Ambitious Woman's Guide to a Successful Career*. Saranac Lake, NY: AMACOM Books, 1980.

Howell, William S., and Ernest G. Bormann, *Presentational Speaking for Business and the Professions*. New York: Harper & Row, 1971.

Jackson, Tom, *Guerrilla Tactics in the Job Market*. New York: Bantam Books, 1978.

Jackson, Tom, and Davidyne Mayleas, *The Hidden Job Market*. New York: Quandrangle/New York Times, 1981.

Karrass, Chester, *Give And Take: The Complete Guide to Negotiating Strategies and Tactics.* New York: T.Y. Crowell, 1974.

Karrass, Chester, *Negotiating Game: How To Get What You Want.* New York: T.Y. Crowell, 1970.

Kennedy, Marilyn Moats, *Career Knockouts: How to Battle Back.* New York: Warner Books, 1982.

Kennedy, Marilyn Moats, *Office Politics: Seizing Power, Wielding Clout.* Chicago: Follett Publishing Co., 1980.

Korda, Michael, *Power! How to Get It, How to Use It.* New York: Random House, 1975.

Korda, Michael, *Success! How Every Man and Woman Can Achieve It.* New York: Random House, 1977.

Kram, Kathy E., *Mentoring Processes at Work: Developmental Relationships in Managerial Careers.* Glenview, IL: Scott Foresman, 1985.

Lainson, Suzanne, *Crash Course.* New York: G.P. Putnam, 1985.

Lakein, Alan, *How to Get Control of Your Time in Your Life.* New York: New American Library, 1974.

LeBoeuf, Michael, *Working Smart.* New York: Warner Books, 1979.

Leiding, Oscar, *A Layman's Guide to Successful Publicity.* Bala Cynwyd, PA: Ayer Press, 1979.

McCormack, Mark H., *What They Don't Teach You at Harvard Business School.* New York: Bantam Books, 1984.

Machlowitz, Marilyn, *Inside Moves*. Boulder: Career Track Publications, 1985.

Machlowitz, Marilyn, *Success at an Early Age*. New York: Arbor House, 1984.

MacKenzie, R. Alec, *New Time Management Methods*. Chicago: Dartnell Publishers, 1978.

Mandino, Og, *The Greatest Salesman in the World*. New York: Frederick Fell, 1968.

Molloy, John T., *Dress for Success*. New York: Warner Books, 1979.

Newman, James A., and Roy Alexander, *Climbing the Corporate Matterhorn*. New York: John Wiley & Sons, 1984.

Norback, Craig T., *Check Yourself Out: The Complete Book of Self-Testing*. New York: Times Books, 1980.

O'Brien, Richard, *Publicity: How to Get It*. New York: Harper & Row, 1977.

Parkhurst, William, *How to Get Publicity*. New York: Times Books, 1984.

Payne, Richard A., *How to Get a Better Job Quicker*. New York: Taplinger Publishing, 1979.

Peale, Dr. Norman Vincent, *The Power of Positive Thinking*. New York: Walker & Company, 1984.

Posner, Mitchell J., *Executive Essentials*. New York: Avon, 1982.

Rawlinson, J.G., *Creative Thinking and Brainstorming*. New York: John Wiley & Sons, 1981.

Ringer, Robert J., *Winning Through Intimidation*. Beverly Hills: Los Angeles Book Publishers, 1973.

Rodman, George, *Speaking Out: Message Preparation for Professionals*. New York: Holt, Rinehart, and Winston, 1978.

Rust, H. Lee, *Jobsearch: A Complete Guide to Successful Job Changing*. New York: AMACOM Books, 1979.

Schatzki, Michael, and Wayne R. Coffey, *Negotiation: The Art of Getting What You Want*. New York: New American Library, 1981.

Stevens, Art, *The Persuasion Explosion*. Washington, DC: Acropolis Books, 1984.

Thompson, Jacqueline, *Image Impact for Men*. New York: Dodd, Mead, 1983.

Traxel, Robert G., *Manager's Guide to Successful Job Hunting*. New York: McGraw-Hill, 1978.

Uris, Auren, and John J. Tarrant, *Career Stages: Surmounting the Crises of Working Life*. New York: G.P. Putnam, 1983.

Wareham, John, *Secrets of a Corporate Head Hunter*, New York: Atheneum, 1980.

Weiner, Richard, *Professional's Guide to Public Relations Services*. New York: Public Relations Publishing, 1980.

Weinstein, Bob, *Jobs for the 21st Century*. New York: Macmillan, 1983.

Welch, Mary Scott, *Networking*. New York: Warner Books, 1980.

Winston, Stephanie, *The Organized Executive*. New York: Warner Books, 1983.

Zey, Michael G., *Mentor Connection*. Chicago: Dow Jones-Irwin, 1984.

Index

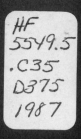